Go Away Closer

How Foreign Travel Stirs a Passion for Local Missions

Elizabeth Barnard

Parson's Porch Books

Go Away Closer: How Foreign Travel Stirs a Passion for Local Missions

ISBN: Softcover 978-0692639368
Copyright © 2015 by Elizabeth Barnard

All rights reserved. No part of this book may be reproduced or transmitted in any form or by any means, electronic or mechanical, including photocopying, recording, or by any information storage and retrieval system, without permission in writing from the publisher.

To order additional copies of this book, contact:

Parson's Porch Books
1-423-475-7308
www.parsonsporch.com

Parson's Porch Books is an imprint of Parson's Porch & Company (PP&C) in Cleveland, Tennessee. PP&C is an innovative company which raises money by publishing books of noted authors, representing all genres. All donations from contributors and profits from publishing are shared with the poor.

Go Away Closer

Acknowledgements

To Mom and Dad
Your love and support goes beyond all reason.

For Vester Boone and Jeff Ward
It's because of people like you, doing what you do locally and abroad people like me become inspired.

For all of those who have joined with me in this journey to make this dream a reality, words cannot express my gratitude and heart felt appreciation of staying with me through this struggle to make this bucket list item a reality. For wonderful editors like Burwell and Sara who tirelessly looked over this with me and I hope I made the proper corrections, thank you. If there are mistakes in the book it is not their fault.

To Life Group, Community Group, church, family, friends, and especially Ashley, Sarah and Andrew for dealing with me while writing, thank you. To the writers and contributors found in this book and the ones who prayed with me along the way, thank you.

Thank you for each of you being you, and allowing God to use your gifts to touch my life.

Foreword

How it all started!

It is really hard for me to know where to begin on this journey that calls me so often to go, be and do. Each part of the circle of missions near, and abroad has contributed to me being literally well rounded. The depth in which I am able to see things locally and the breadth in which I have been able to see things internationally brings me back into the circle at different places all of the time. It is within this complex world that I find the idea of "doing what you are called to do where you are called to do it" so important. At different points in my life, I have focused in different areas, and that is the nature of life itself, ebbing and flowing us different areas and down different streams where we may stay for a while. Then all of a sudden the current of life picks back up and takes us to a new place, a place unknown, a place where we have to resettle, refigure, and restate our ideas, hopes, and dreams, aware of our past failures, fears, and faults.

Working with nonprofits and volunteering was ingrained in me when I was young. The constant urge to help someone when they were in need was not something that was just felt in my family; it was something that I was so blessed to see acted upon day in and day out. This allowed me to understand the importance of seeing needs consistently, but nothing ever was complete. This among other occurrences was the tipping point to start my constant concern and dialogue about non-profits, the way they function and how to network with other people and other non-profits.

So from as early as I can remember, I worked multiple weeks at various bible schools-sometimes three and four different bible schools in the summer. Then I was able to help others with various medical, social and economic needs. Being willing and able to help out with all different types of situations allowed me to build a platform and network of people and places who care about the areas around them and have a passion to encourage, equip, and empower those they work with on a regular basis. This allowed me to be inspired about ways in which I can be a resource to others when they do not have the foundation that I have been blessed to create and maintain.

From this passion I was able to see that this was a need wherever I went. From traveling down the road to large cities, then traveling regionally and internationally the need for networking and relationships became more and more prevalent to me. There was an understanding that we are made for community. We are made to bring God close to us, and us close to Him. Ways which are often difficult to navigate with others, many times bring the best results. These results create bonds that are not easily broken. When we encourage others, we help them walk towards areas that they may not approach alone, but that God is calling them to. When we equip others, we teach them how to fish instead of giving them fish, providing for them in a way that is not a handout, but becomes a hand up out of whatever poverty or oppression they are in, even if it is self-induced. When we empower, we give others the vision to see past their barriers and set new goals, dream new dreams and shoot for the stars in ways that they never thought possible. We motivate one who never had shoes to give shoes to millions: we encourage one who never had a dream to spark a change in the world. We empower the least of these to be the voices for the voiceless, the hope in a lost world, and the light in a dark place. I want to be that type of person.

I started a blog a long time ago tagged EB3- EB for my initials and the three meaning these three E's; Equip, Empower, and Encourage. I took it a step further and wanted to start a non-profit at the time, called H.O.M.E. Though this is an acronym, this word had so much meaning for me. I was always encouraged as a child to call the place I lived a home-not because it was a specific building but because those who lived under the roof were people that I loved and cherished. When I would say I would come to the house, I would be gently corrected to say that I was coming home. This had more of an impact than I realized. This home was where I was loved, where I was cared for, where I was 100% me - the good, the bad, the ugly, the spastic, the annoyed, you get the picture. This was the place where everything could be falling apart or everything could fit perfectly, and either way, I was going to be loved and cared for through it. I still have this home now, and it is a pure joy knowing that this is possible on earth. I can only imagine what God's home is going to be like. If I have it this good now, what could be better? I can see lost loved ones have a "big big house, with lots and lots of rooms," a song reference for all of those who grew up in the 90's in church. There would be a love that would undeniably surround me.

What home are you going to after your time here is done? Maybe my story of a home life is only your fairy tale. Maybe you were on the other side and wherever you lived was never a home. Maybe nothing came even remotely close to a home where you could be open and honest with who you were and those who lived under the same roof. For that I am sorry. I don't begin to understand your pain or your hurt, but I do understand that there is a God that is greater than that. There is a God who is good, who wants you to come home, who wants you to be real and who wants to hold you, love you and never leave you. Remember you are not HOME yet.

The acronym for the HOME is Helping Others Motivate Everyone. Though it is not the non-profit that I thought it would be, God is currently taking me on a different course. He is shaping my story though this lens. If we are to be the body that Christ calls us to be, then we are called to help others learn, follow, and celebrate their walk and relationship with Himself and with one another. How we do this is through our different talents and gifts that God has given us, and not out of a requirement by God for a works-based mentality, but out of our love and overflowing joy for following and obeying his commands.

At church we have this vision that happens behind our missions. It is something that we have recently switched to and something that I think God is blessing through the ways in which we have tried to approach life and our relationships with other people.

We have been called to be a lighthouse to a dark and broken world. God is telling us that he should be center of lives and as George, one of our executive pastors, says "that he should not just be center, but that God should be the epicenter of our lives." A lighthouse provides light and hope to those who are in need of it, and the lighthouse also provides wisdom and guidance during a time when direction and understanding can often be null and void in this crazy world. Each lighthouse is differing slightly as they are spaced around the coasts all across the world. They each carry the same message, but in a slightly different format. The pattern on the lighthouse, as well as the light pattern itself, helps the sailors tell them apart so they know where they are. If you are using a lighthouse for direction, you are in conditions that are not ideal for sailing. There is not a sun that is blaring outside on a clear calm and beautiful day. The view from the bow of the boat is not pristine or picturesque. The time when lighthouses are needed is when the conditions are not ideal. The waters and winds are rough enough that the ships directional capabilities are not what they could be and despite the best sailor's efforts, things are getting turned around.

We find ourselves in these situations on a regular basis. There are things in life that we find ourselves in over and over again. Situations that we think never could happen to us, have left us crippled, not knowing who, what or where to turn to. Yet there is always God present in the midst of it all, acting as our lighthouse, our city on a hill, our burning bush and our flame of hope. It is only when we focus on the lighthouse closely enough that we can see the lighthouse we are near. Do you ever feel this way with God, that there is a specific type of discernment that we are looking for and the storm is raging around us? It is when we focus intently on the lighthouse that we find a solution. Our storms don't seem so big and we can see a way out of it. It is always when the storms are raging in our lives that the seas are rough and then we can easily get focused on the things that are right in front of us. Yet when we look out a little further, we see that there is hope, there is guidance, and there is one who knows where the obstructions are in the path that we are on, and how to avoid them.

It is important to pay attention to the reasons that we begin serving. We need to focus on what our assumptions are at the beginning of the process and pay attention to the ways we are molded and shaped as we continue serving. It is through our serving and life instances that we are challenged and are forced to evaluate our serving, our service to others, and those we serve. It is important to remember that we are changed through our encounters, and our mission focus so too is also changed, challenged and pushed in ways we never thought possible at any level. It is my prayer that through scripture, God's call on your life, my experiences and others that you can find your own way of "going away closer".

Introduction

Certainly travel is more than just a seeing of sights: it is a change that goes on, deep and permanent in the ideas of living.

- Anonymous

I remember it vividly and I bet my parents do, too. We were celebrating my birthday on the porch of our house that hot summer day. I don't remember people being around, just the three of us as we sat and reflected on the many changes that were going to come within the coming months. There was a tension in the air much like an elephant in the room, one that may have seemed daunting, but one that was inevitably coming very soon. For this elephant was college. I had decided to go to the school that was the farthest in the state from my house. This choice was not made by geographical facts but by what I thought God was calling me to study, and the beach.

I found out later that God would change my plans and my major multiple times. I came to soon realize I was an eternal student. However, this did not change the fact that this hot summer day I was caught between the rock that I had known at home and the hard place that I was assuming college would be. So there I sat in that old metal rocking chair on my front porch with presents on both sides and getting down to the last present. I took a deep breath. I had been told to hold this present for later, but I was not sure why. Opening it up, I noticed something green and soft and pulling it out, I saw that it was a blanket of the college that I would be attending.

If you are like me, there are certain things for to for personal and sentimental reasons: that we get attached. A piece of paper that someone you once knew wrote or drew on, a picture that is terrible, but which reminds you of a time "way back when", or a shirt with 1,000 holes that somehow you just have to hold onto because it has become more than an item. They have become memories. This is the immediate feeling I had about this blanket. I pulled it out and inspected the sides. One side was slick, and the other side was fleece, perfect for the hot and cold nature that I knew I could expect ahead.

Then there was a corner, a corner that was different than the rest, and on that corner was a saying that I will never forget. "Go Away Closer" was embroidered on the edge of this blanket, a saying that up until then I had never even heard. I would not have understood if I had.

This saying quickly became embedded within my heart. This was not my parent's sly way of trying to get me to transfer schools to less than 4.5 hours away (or maybe it was). It was a reminder that even if I go away, I will always be close to them. After a few tears were shed, because we knew what was coming, we spent the rest of the day just enjoying one another's company. Life was good and the blanket was ready for its first adventure to school. Yet, the saying was already impacting, molding, and making me who I am today.

School came and went with the various scars and successes. My major changed once officially, yet unofficially four times. Over the course of my four years, living on campus I had more than fourteen suitemates-roommates. College was the epitome of change. Graduation came, then work followed. During that time the blanket stayed by my side. I remember quitting a job after college, for numerous reasons, but mainly to attend graduate school. I started at one school, ending up transferring to another school, and the second school was the best decision of my life. The admissions coordinator not only listened to my requests, but also worked with me through the transitions.

You are probably thinking that this story is all about a blanket and its travels. That is not even close. The blanket, although mentioned later in the book, is not the key focus. The blanket is among the countless testimonies that declare of God's goodness and blessing, and the countless ways that He has called us to "Go Away Closer." This book is divided into four sections properly named, Go, Away, Closer and ",". The last one may seem odd, but I am of the belief that we should never put a period where God is trying to put a comma in our lives.

This is just my story; I pray that you will be mindful of how God is writing your story as you "Go Away Closer." I hope you enjoy the stories and find that some of the experiences shine a light on moments in which God has moved and has been working in and through you and your life. I will be praying for you as you take the next steps and continue on the journey with me, but most importantly with Him.

Many thoughts and prayers,

Elizabeth

A Challenging Beginning

"An individual has not started living until he can rise above the narrow confines of his individualistic concerns to the broader concerns of all humanity."

-Martin Luther King Jr.

Beginning is always a challenging concept for me. Where to begin is often the hardest part. I am a "big picture" type of person, most of the time. Therefore, when it comes to the details of how and where I am supposed to start a project, I sometimes get lost. When the idea of a book was on the bucket list, I had a passion to accomplish and create something that was meaningful and made an impact.

What can I write about that makes a difference and causes one to think, and yet in a way can give back to the greater good? Chris wrote about world domination and how to achieve this concept. He states: "If you want it badly enough, are willing to make some changes in your life to cause it to happen, you too can take over the world...or do anything else you really want to do... Yes, you really can have it all. The only things you'll need to give up are assumptions, expectations, and the comfort zone that holds you back from greatness." [1]

I have a passion for travel, for seeing the world through the eyes of the One who created it, in all its richness and beauty. I have a passion for people, and I have a passion to help others find what they are passionate about and pursue their goals. I am typically unconventional in my methods, having held more jobs and random positions than I could count, and meeting more people and being blessed by more stories than I could ever write about. In this book I hope to pair my travels and others with my encounters with God. In my time on earth, I have focused on life in a different way, a way that may not be seen as "normal." Being unashamedly independent, thanks to my Fourth of July birthdate as well as my "only child"

---

[1] (Guillebeau,4).

nature, I find joy in figuring out what the world has for each of us, if we are willing to take time out and smell the roses.

What do you really want to get out of life? What can you offer the world that no one else can? "For far too long, we have failed to recognize the importance of each of these mindsets together doing what you really want and radically helping others." The problem is that in the prevailing logic of our modern age, these two perspectives have traditionally been viewed as opposites. You can do something good for yourself, or you can do something good for other people. ... but wait a second. Why can't you do something great for others while you are out changing the world for good"[2]

So here goes, here are my stories, my encounters with scripture, God, and others and how they each allow me to see the world in a new and brighter way. I pray that as we first take a look at how the scriptures tell us to go and the way in which a few of my favorite characters show their obedience and even disobedience to God and His call, that we can find a hint of similar qualities within each one of us.

There are times when we each want to obey but stay away from the things that God is calling us to do because we fear the unknown. We have the fear of failure, and the fear of just *change*. God calls us to change, to transition, try something new, to create, to move, and shake the world for His name and His renown, and that is what I hope and pray and intend to do. This is a cycle that ebbs and flows with the passing of time and the changing of life. We get called to go on a global mission, called to serve locally and then called sometimes to do both or something in between. Let's take a deeper look and investigate how He calls us to go, and where He has led people in the past, giving us encouragement to be led in the future. John Stott states that "We must be global Christians with a global vision because our God is a global God."

---

[2] (Guillebeau, 13).

Yearning for More

"It is not about how much money you earn or what job you have. That is not what people remember... all the greats did something for the world."

- Ashley Vestal '

God woke me up this morning hungry. This may seem strange or normal, depending on who you talk to, but this was weird for me this morning. Not only was work cancelled because of ice the night before; no alarm was set, and I had no scheduled programming. This does not usually happen in my life. Add to that the fact that for the past two weeks I have been dealing with tremendous anxiety, acid reflux, and stomach issues that have me sleeping and not hungry. Well, not this morning. Up before 5 and eating a protein bar. I was literally hungry and awake. He was calling me to listen and to be in His presence. Since I had already shoved food in my mouth, I decided to read a book that I started the night before - one in which I had read before but I knew it would be good to read again. This book was "Crazy Love" by Francis Chan. If you have not read or listened to Chan, please go do yourself a favor and listen to him. The way God uses him to articulate His word and His vision for so many lives is astounding.

So not to my surprise, I was caught up in the web of scriptures and stories that were being woven within this book. I saw myself in so many different areas of life: where I came from, what my relationship with God looked like at one point, to what it is now, to what I want it to be in the future. All of these thoughts began to swarm and swim in my head. What is my purpose? What is my meaning? To be honest, I don't think I will ever know how my purpose and meaning will be lived out but I do know that my purpose and meaning is to know God and to make Him known. With that knowledge, I am then entrusted to do something about it.

There is something about radical obedience that calls, compels, and thrusts us not only into a relationship with God, but a relationship with others. How are we living this call? I along with so many others have hopped on the bandwagon of reading the books that call us to be radical about our faith and our lives. It is something that inspires me and moves me closer to where I feel God is leading me. Yet I see it with myself and others time and time again that we read, read, and read and NOTHING is ever done.

We fall into the trap of this lukewarm water and it is so boring and dull, and leaves no impact at all. This is the call that we have to change the water temperature. What are we doing that shows people we need to leave some habits cold and frozen in their tracks? Where are we making an impact that is so hot it is literally blazing a trail so that new people to the faith don't question where we are going, but see where we have been? When you think of hot or cold water, there are literal feelings that become associated with these two. For the hot, many think sweating, reddening of skin, faster heart rate; but then you get into the extremes if you are in the heat for too long. The same but opposite factors happen in the cold. You turn a certain color. You shake to stay warm. Your teeth may chatter. The hairs on your arms stand up. Your heart is trying to heat your body. You naturally are drawn to the warmth. God is that warmth. We are called to draw near to him -a selfish, glorious God wanting only what is best for us and giving that to us, Himself. Yet, we distance ourselves from where He calls us. We drive those thoughts away, because they are not a part of the status quo, the society standard, the neighborhood regulations, or they are just plain weird.

In my story the lists of jobs that I have held both paid and not is rather long. The positions I have held vary in different fields and vocations. Many cases I have been introduced as Elizabeth and she does "yea". Then I was described as someone who does banking, or a veterinarian or something that can be described in one phrase, but better yet one word. I initially was truly annoyed with the "yea" as my job title. I had jobs with titles, but because they were multiple, it was condensed into "yea." This was often followed by "She is random and so are her many jobs." To me it represented a society failure, something which I was supposed to accomplish, but was "still working towards" or something that I needed to do to seem complete. I could not have been further from that mentality. Many times the articulation of my myriad jobs seemed to take me longer to spell out than people wanted to hear. I would just say one of the three, or five or however many I had at the time and smile and move the conversation on because I knew it wouldn't truly matter.

While I was in training for a leadership course, the class was asked by the guest speaker to describe who they were from 9-5 and 5-9. This concept was to help her get to know the students. It allowed us creativity in describing who we are, what we do, and why we do it. As each student went around the room, words and phrases were spoken that described each person. There were some stereotypical answers of husband, mother, pastor, and then some answers arose which invoked passion. Some mentioned being a voice for the oppressed, or hope for the broken. When it was my turn to speak all I could say was I was a "mission-minded random job holder." This describes my core beliefs. It does not matter what job I hold. What matters is the way I leverage my talents and skills to how God wants to use me.

Have you ever felt that way about something? Do you have something that you are passionate about that confines your entire day and you could spend an entire afternoon talking to someone about your passion? This talk would just scratch the surface of what you love and how it impacts you. People often within the first two minutes begin to turn a deaf ear to the conversation and make a mental note never to ask you about it again. If so, then you feel my pain.

Sometimes there are a select few people who get inspired or inspire you and your passion. When you find those people, never let them go. These are the ones that inspire conversations that turn into brainstorming hours of insight and often conviction of purpose. These conversations lead to inspiration, hope, and commitment to the project and passion more than you had previously.

God gave me this "yea" not singular job holding title so I could be in the margins - so I could make the bridges and attempt to build the network that is called both missions and His church. People question my going to divinity school when I did not want to be a traditional preacher and preach every Sunday or work in a church on a consistent basis. I do believe however, that daily we preach whether that is our professional job or not. Though I work through the church and its people, I do not think it is necessary to have a church building where only in these confines do you live out a life worthy of Christ. I am not saying that I do not think it is extremely important for you to be a part of a church body where not only you can worship but have people who you "pour into" and they pour into you, because that is EXTREMELY important. I am saying you don't have to be in a church to be a minister. We need ministers within every work base. It can be within a 9-5 job in corporate America or a 24-hour job of being a mom or dad. You are being a minister to someone whether you realize it or not.

I have "preached" more outside of the church than within it. I am not talking about the prepared preaching that we were taught how to do in divinity school. God gifted some amazing people to do that. I have witnessed, been a part, and been impacted by these sermons and ministers. I am talking about the recognition that God is living and active in our lives and in our world on a daily basis. While in preaching class, we were taught and had to write the ways in which we saw God moving in and through the world at large. It could be something big, or something small, but how we saw God displaying himself to His people. These were called sermon introductions or ways to pull the audience we were talking to into the story God was using us to tell.

That same type of sermon introduction is the encompassing work of this book. God has pulled me over and over into missions, and He still does. This is my introduction to His story, not my ending. The way He uses each of us in our own way is breathtaking. We preach as we express our priorities, being kind or unpleasant to the ones on the street, compassionate or condemning to those who entrust us with their problems, get mad at the person in the drive through, impatient with our parents and/or children. Trust me, we preach enough. Is our preaching making a difference? Is it creating a way that others can see where we are going and what our drive is? Is it drawing us closer to God and His will for our lives?

The decisions that we make on how, when, where to live should be articulated through Christ and His word. He wants to spend time with us. He values us. He loves us. Our response to Him is so often avoidance, complacency, disregard, or frustration. Missions near or far beckons us or calls us to draw from a source that is outside of ourselves. This source is never empty and never will run dry and is one that is full of hope, grace, love and redemption. It is this source, which mission provides that when listened to and obeyed provokes a change in our hearts. (Out of our hearts our mouths speak (verse).

Over and over and OVER within the scriptures we are called to set a fire, to blaze a trail, to make a path, and to use the gifts and characteristics that God gave us. We have to be lights for Him. God led Moses and his people during the exodus by a pillar of fire at night (Exodus 13:21). God says also that our work will be made evident by fire, testing the quality of our work (1 Corinthians 3:13). Then God uses fire to relate back to Himself, saying that he is the all-consuming fire found in Hebrews 12:29. What a great reminder that God wants us to be consumed with Him alone. We should be so caught up in the grace, redemption and yearning for knowledge in Christ that we are a consuming fire, one that can't help but be noticed, can't help but blaze a trail, and can't help but be a light in dark places.

How are we spending our time? Are we told we are at church too much? Are we told to stop giving because we have already given over what we are called to do? Do people see us as givers or takers?

"Go away closer" requires us to think outside of the norm, out of the box, away from the principle that we need to leverage what we have to our greatest ability. This is a huge asset and requirement when we see God moving and working in our life.

"We worship a God who specialized in resurrection. He specializes in hopeless situations."[3] What are the areas of hopeless situations that we see in our lives and that we encounter on mission trips and bring home with us? At some point we must enter this reality that we need to understand the importance of having a void because this warrants the importance of having a solution.

---

[3] (Wilson, 169).

I was standing in the shower after a quick trip to the gym this evening. Yes, I know what you are thinking, we are all happy that I showered. However sometimes light bulbs happen when you least expect them. It was a cold day today and I had been bundled up all day. I wore a scarf inside and I was in my bedroom shoes all day because I did not have to work. It was a great concept yet going to the gym required me to change and pull out the sweatpants and the sweatshirt and tennis shoes and head over there. (Missions require us to change out of our normal routine). My workout at the gym was quick tonight, working on just a few minutes to get up to burning the amount of calories that I wanted to burn, then out the door in time to take a quick shower at home before going over to a friend's house later this evening.

Hurrying, I hopped in the shower and turned the water on hot. It does not take long to get warm because the water heater is directly under my bathroom. All of the sudden I realized how cold I had been all day without even really paying attention. (We get stuck in spiritual ruts without knowing it) The hot water felt like the world's best sauna and it was created in that moment just for me to stand there and just see the steam rising from the water as it came out of the shower head.

Ok, you get the picture. However, all of a sudden the thought ran through my head that if this water was recycled over and over again just to pour back on my head, that would be wonderful. It would not be going down the drain to oblivion. At this moment I could not bear the thought of wasting the hot water that was feeling so great at the time. I know this may sound trivial to many of you. I can't even enjoy a hot shower without feeling guilty? Well, for me the answer is no.

I am not saying that everyone is not supposed to enjoy a hot shower, but God speaks to me so much through water. It is in the stillness or the rough nature of the waves at the ocean that I see His presence and hear His voice. It is in the water bottle that I am forced to carry with me on mission trips. In certain locations they are not privileged enough to have water they can drink right out of the tap or out of a well, because they don't have a faucet. It is in the waterfalls that were crafted long before I was ever thought about and will remain long after I have passed on that I see His beauty, His creation, His majesty. It is in the little drip that I hear from the shower that makes me get out of bed at night to turn the knobs tighter so I will not waste water. It is the turning off of the water while I brush my teeth, because that water is also precious. It is in the awe and beauty that I find in organizations that are committed to bringing water to areas which are in such great need and one of the reasons that I am so passionate about recycling water bottles, because they at one point held something that was so important to life.

My revelation in the shower at that moment was that we all have our individual causes that we champion. Each person has something that we have a passion for and things that make us upset when we see them not being cared for properly. We were made for a purpose. For some, it might be stopping people from littering (another thing that gets me because it goes into our water systems). For others it could be human trafficking. People are concerned with shoes for bare feet, homes for the homeless, care for the elderly. Others advocate for only buying clothes made in your country to support your country's economic growth, only chocolate from a certain company, or support for our veterans. There are as many facets to support as there are problems. The list of things we care about is inexhaustible, but that is the beauty of it. If we all cared about those people getting water, then we would have everyone without water and no one with homes. If all we cared about were people who don't have shoes, then who is helping the elderly or those being trafficked?

No cause is greater than the other. It is about the motive that is behind the cause that we move to our "Go Away Closer" status. From this we see that lives are being changed by the things that we do. Our lives become living examples to the world around us. We preach a life worthy of preaching that creates positive change. People are watching each of us all the time. Though this may seem scary, it is a great accountability to which we should, and I hope we do, hold each other.

Will we fail?

Absolutely.

Can we rise?

Of course.

It is called grace. It is the most amazing thing that Christ gave us, when He died for each of us. We fail, we always have and we always will. He loved us enough not to count us unredeemable and to die for each one of us individually. This means that we will still fail even when we try not to, but that we are made clean. Cleaner than any hot shower could ever make us. We are forgiven because of the debt he paid.

It is through the people that we meet along the way that we find either with similar passions or different passions, with the same motives, that we can spur or encourage another as we grow and walk. From these groups we can be called to a higher place. We can be called to something we never even thought we could accomplish and would not be able to on our own. We could be called or requested to move to an area where we did not know or speak the language. God may use us to move to an area in our hometown that is lower income than we are, but we know we are there to make a difference.

What is the calling, the passion, that keeps you up at night? What type of pictures do you have around your house? I heard that you do not have to ask a person what is important to them. If you watch what they take pictures of and what photos they have continuously around their house, you will soon find out. I began to look at my life through this lens. I had never thought about this before. It was something that didn't really cross my mind up to this point. I liked taking pictures for the sake of taking pictures (I thought). When I truly sat down and thought about this, I found that many of the pictures that I take (if not 90 percent or more) are of people. Most of the times my pictures are of people at a specific place to bring up a memory. This is what I love.

If you come in my house, there are pictures of friends, family, and mission trip people all around my house. My kitchen is filled with children from Belize. My living room and dining room are both decorated with friends and family. Then mixed in with these pictures are pictures of landscapes or buildings from my travel that spark memories of places and the moments that I had with certain people all throughout my life. What may look like a leaf with a raindrop on my wall might be just that. It might also be the breakthrough of a student who during the entire mission trip was missing the point of what it was all about. When I gave the student my camera to take a picture of me and some friends in a certain area, he began taking pictures of the way that he saw God in nature. He came up to me a little while later and showed me the leaf pictures. He told me what it meant to him. That was his breakthrough. We all have those moments, and I choose to frame mine.

I have met people over and over again, who have great ideas. They have thought about something for weeks, months, or even years, and they have come up with something that in their minds, will truly change the world. Sometimes it might be as crazy an idea as Apple being the new leader in technology, or whatever is the next big thing is in their field. I, too, have fallen into this trap. I call this the "idea world." We each have ideas and want to see them turn into something wonderful.

The problem is most of the time we do nothing with our ideas. We get caught in this trap of this "idea world" over and over again. Often we say, "I am going to make a difference," and set out to be the light in an area. Then we allow time and other priorities to slip in between that and what will change the world. This concept used to plague me. Why couldn't my ideas, all of my ideas be awesome? I kept changing them, never focusing on one, but on the pursuit of many. This was compounded by the fact that my experiences were not the same as those of another. It shook me and made me mad. I seemed to be getting nowhere by society's standards or my own. Then I realized I needed to change the standards by which I was measuring.

If an idea is so important to me, I should be doing something about it. If we believe in our ideas so much, why are we not putting forth the effort to make that difference and to be that change? Gandhi said it best when he declared, "Be the change you wish to see in the world." This was followed in by a great quote by Manny Okonma. Manny calls us to something higher, something different and something out of the ordinary, when he says, "Do common things in uncommon ways and you will gain the attention of the world."

This phrase is one that is painted and framed on my wall. This simple phrase has changed by vision, my perspective, and my passion. I love looking at ordinary things and flipping them in ways and for uses that are unconventional and not normal.

My life is uncommon. There is no person alive who has had all the same experiences, conversations, and thoughts that I have had. That is a wonderful thought. With this knowledge, I can then share my opinion and experiences with others to make a change and impact in their lives just like so many others have made in mine over the years. The smallest words put together have created the largest impact in my life. These words have come from friends, enemies, family, professors, and books. These, all compiled together to form my current reality. This is what makes my story important, just like it makes your story important. New chapters to my story are being added regularly. I am still reaching for new goals and new dreams. Things keep getting added on my bucket list daily. There are times when I get the pure joy of crossing them off. Sometimes I get caught up in the need to cross items off my list. When this happens, I often miss the picture of the journey that is created in attempting to reach the goal. Sometimes the biggest moments are made from little moments continuously added upon each other. The end of the journey is often trumped by the journey itself.

There is this goal, this desire, this aspiration to be willing, able, and accessible for God. Let Him use me when and how He sees fit to make a difference in the life of one or lives of many. This is what ultimately drives everything else. How can my passion better equip you to be the best you, can be? How can my passion help improve the world in which I live, and the greater world at large? To be honest, I don't know. I am still figuring that out. I believe that I will always be processing that. However, I believe that God will change my passions to fit His purpose whenever, and however needed, if I just listen.

I spent some of my time living in the shadows of other people, trying to be normal. The one who has the same job, the same travel, the same everything. This might work for you. This might be the way that God is using you to make His impact on your family, in your neighborhood and the relationships that you have fostered over the years. Your "closer" is unique only to you. However, my normal has been thrown out the window as I embrace the different person that God is calling me to be.

As each of us is impacted by the world around us, we have a choice as to how to impact the world. If we go on trips that change us, or find new realities that we did not know about the world around us, our lives are forced to change. We are forced to look at our homes differently, and we have a choice to make. Are you going to do something with and about what you have learned or are you going to ignore the change that occurred within your life and your heart and go on being ordinary? You are fearfully and wonderfully made. My dream is to use what I have in the best way I can, and be happy with it. For this time, too, shall pass. How are you leveraging your wonder, your dream for Him and His kingdom?

I am glad that God has called me to something different, not better, not higher, but different. God knew that a "normal" life by American standards was not in my deck of cards, He knew that I would be hard-headed, a school nerd, and have this passion to meet people from all over the world. He knew I would want to learn and hear their stories attempting to see things through their eyes. He created me this way. After I began to better understand who I was within Christ, and who He created me to be personally, things changed. I no longer cared as much about trying to fit into the neat box or the status quo. I finally had the guts to cast away the "me" that was hindering my own progress and find the person (as I still find more daily) He is calling me to be.

Take time to think about stories that have molded and impacted you. Some are probably a mixture of good and bad, but they made you who you are today. You are not defined by them, but your vision is molded by them. If you want the vision to change, it can't change on its own. Focus on stories in which you have impacted others, and moments and times when things have impacted you, and brought you to your knees, or to a place of renewal or new perspective. I pray that these times do not scare you or trap you in a state of nostalgia. I pray that they allow you to be open to the possibility of whatever He is going to do in and through you next.

Finding your passion and purpose is not an easy thing. It is not something that many people can just sit down and articulate. When asked that question for the first time we find that images are hard to conjure. "What is your purpose?", sometimes renders a blank response. The passion of your life deserves a fire and drive that you can visibly see. As a whole, society is lacking in these areas. We have confined ourselves to being ordinary, to being mundane, and to being mediocre. When we push against this idea of non-conformity we are then held back by our own fears of failure and struggles along with others doubts.

I do believe that we were not meant to succeed on the first try, though some have the joy of succeeding initially. I believe that we fail initially when we try something new as a test to see if we are willing to get back up and fight for that idea again. Our failure often is not because of lack of effort or preparation, but we learn from our mistakes and we grow. We are strengthened by our encounters that were successful in the midst of chaos. Society isn't set up to allow "non-normal" success easily. Society wasn't prepared for a Savior the way in which He came, ministered, lived and impacted, either. Who will we choose to be like?

When we have to fight the society standards to attempt to make a difference, this is the chasm in which our world changing ideas often get lost. I was talking with my roommate about this the other night. Many times our conversations turn into vision casting or encouraging sessions for each other. We talk about what the future should look like and what it would take to make that happen. Many times we question our current roles and where we think God is calling us.

While talking, the quote "If you want to be somebody, if you want to go somewhere, you better wake up and pay attention" popped into our conversation. This throws me back to the scene in *Sister Act II* where they are at a pivotal moment in the story. *Sister Act II*, is one of my all-time favorite movies, starring Whoopi Goldberg. A Catholic school deems it necessary to rebuild a broken community through the use of a choir composed of underprivileged youth. That is the short version of the story. Led by Whoopi, a Las Vegas show girl turned nun, they have the choice to hide in the shadows and not share their gifts or they have the choice to stand out, to make a difference and to amount to something. I believe often many of these pivotal moments in our lives leave us at a crossroad. This crossroad is where we have to come to terms with the reality that we either have to make a change, take a stand, and dare to be against the status quo. If this doesn't happen we have to be ok with the reality that we will remain the same.

I go back to the quote at the beginning of the chapter: Each great person we know lived a life of action. I racked my brain thinking about people whom I consider to be great. Both the names of prominence and those personal heroes in our own lives, hold special places in our hearts. I hope it is different for each one of us. Abraham Lincoln was equipped with the courage necessary to complete the task of leading the United States through the Civil War. Through this process, he was able to abolish slavery, bolster the economy and strengthen the federal government. There was courage spoken through adversity to say that "In the end, it's not the years of your life that count, but the life in your years." Mother Teresa, Gandhi, Billy Graham, and others all rank highly on my list of influential people. The tenacity that each have or had for life, and the care and consideration they displayed for others exemplified their selfless nature.

All of these greats have something in common. They had highs and lows in life just like each of us do, but it is what they did with those highs and lows that made a difference. They had the potential to see of what could be, not what was or had to be that changed and shaped their outlook and impact in life. Christine Caine, leader of Propel Women and the A21 Campaign which helps reach and rescue women in slavery, reminds us of God needing to have space in our lives to work. She declares,

"[Loosen] up your life enough to be ready for interruptions. Don't structure your days so rigidly that you lock out God from working with you in the middle of them."[4]

---

[4] (Caine).

So many others have shaped and molded my mindset during times of trial and struggle. There are times when these pale in comparison to the drive that I have to change something that matters to me. God wants us available to be ready to work for whatever He calls us to.

How can we come up with ideas and ways to impact society? I am an avid Pinterest freak and there are so many boards that I read to gain ideas and to see how old items that I have lying around the house can be used in new and unconventional ways. One of my favorite things on Pinterest is the quote section. I am an avid reader and according to my best friend, I am partial to the "cheesy" quotes. The quote board that I have has over 100 ideas that are on it and yet I still have more and more that I add to it daily.

One of the best quotes that stays with me is spoken by Eleanor Roosevelt, "Great minds discuss ideas, good minds discuss things and average minds discuss people". Taking this into account into my life, I have seen that over and over, the discussion of ideas yields benefits. I am beyond blessed to have friends and family who discuss ideas on a consistent basis, allowing my mind to be filled with what could be instead of what is.

This concept is compounded by the joy that I get from reading books, blogs, articles both new and old on leadership, management and self-improvement. Some of these reinforce positive behaviors and attitudes in the midst of life's hard times, trials and temptations, and act as inspiration. It is important to begin with scripture and see where we are called to go. The reality that some followed Christ and some did not, brings a great reminder that this is a problem that society as a whole has been dealing with since its inception. The thought that we have the daily, hourly, minute-by-minute choice to make a difference is scary, yet amazingly freeing. We find that with each moment that we are given we have the ability to make the world a better place. What are you doing about that to bring God closer to humanity at large? How are you in your hometown putting passion behind your purpose?

God allows us to be impacted by certain people, places, things and to gain wisdom from our experiences to mold us so that we are available for use when needed. On Pinterest, no two people have the same boards, same pins, just like no two people are the same in their thoughts, actions and characteristics (praise the Lord). If you are a Pinterest frequent visitor, like I am, you will understand that sometimes our five minutes of browsing can turn into an hour of wasted time. This expansion of time proves that we are intrigued by others' interests. It is a part of our human nature. So when we see boards and pins that are different from ours, we are left with a choice to be impacted by its content or not. We impact others in this same manner, in a way that is uniquely our own. Whether that be positive or negative, it allows us to leave a mark on society.

Will we choose to be mutually beneficial?

Is our effect going to last?

Are we going to impact positively or negatively?

The choice is ours alone to make.

What are we leveraging, and willing to leverage in our lives that is going to make a worldly but also an eternal impact? It is hard to see the forest for the trees sometimes. Take a moment to think about the resources that you have. Maybe your resources are financial, physical, or emotional. Take time for just a moment and jot these things down on a sheet of paper. The length of your list does not equate to being a better or more spiritually deep Christian; it just shows you where your passions are. Now as you look at that list, do you see any connections?

Do any of your friends have a few of those same gifts? Write their names alongside of their respective interests. Now is there an area where you are lacking that you would like to have more of? Do you know someone with these skills? Put this in a different section of your paper. This may seem strange and take you a while...I have rewritten my sheet over and over. As my passions, and prerogatives change so too does my heart and where God calls me.

What is your passion?

Where is He calling you to go?

Go

Where Does the Bible Go?

"The Bible is not the basis of missions; missions is the basis of the Bible"

-Ralph Winter, Missiologist

"World missions was on God's mind from the beginning."

-Dave Davidson

What we see within scripture from the people that God uses in both New and Old Testament is to point others towards Him, His love and His word. If we do not go, if we do not bear witness to the things that He has done in our lives, then we leave the field when the harvest is plentiful and the workers are few (Luke 10:2). Too many people have already left the field. It is time that we go and tell the world of this good news.

There are numerous stories within scripture in which God calls us to "go" and do the work He has called us to do. Of all these stories, Joseph from the book of Genesis is one of my favorite stories. Why is this my favorite story? It all started with his coat. Joseph in this story was said to have been given a coat of many colors by his father to display his father's affection for him. Growing up, I loved bold colors. I still do, and I just imagined this coat being awesome. Not only was the coat cool, but the musical "Joseph and the Amazing Technicolor Dream coat" came out on video tape (yep, that's right, VHS) and this was the coolest thing ever to my young mind. My favorite section of scripture was in a musical. My two favorite worlds collided. The movie created by Hollywood is not exactly biblically accurate. However, at this time in my development, it created a yearning for me to know more about this boy Joseph and his story and impact on history.

The difference that God makes in the scriptures when He is talking about Joseph and his journey is shown when Joseph is forced to go away and be sold into slavery, yet he is brought back to take care of his chosen people. The concept of a brother's dream ultimately leading to being sold by his other brothers seems weird. The audacity that the brothers had to cut the coat just baffled me, and I studied and studied these chapters. This may all seem a little out of context, so let me frame the story.

The story of Joseph is found in the first book of the sixty-six books of the Bible. This story takes up more of Genesis than you may think it does, being longer than even some of the Bible's later books. First appearing in chapter 35, 37, and then reappearing in chapter 39 all the way through the end of Genesis in chapter 50, Joseph's story is told Joseph was not where he wanted to be in life. He was not becoming what he thought he was going to be. He came from a big family with eleven other brothers. This created family tensions, as Joseph's mother was his father Jacob's favorite wife. Through circumstances not controlled by Joseph, he was pushed and pulled to different locations, all while living in obedience to him and trusting that God was in control, Joseph was forced to "go" in different directions. He was also led by God to move in obedience to Him and His timing. Joseph used the gifts God had given him to help others along the journey while being obedient to God's timing and placement. This is the life that I would want to have. I would want complete obedience to God and understanding that He is in control in all my situations.

Even though this story is in the first book of the Bible, this is not the first time in scripture that we see someone being told to "go". Chapter three of Genesis, we see Adam and Eve being forced to go. Banished from the Garden of Eden, God forces them to work the land that easily entangles. This was after their eating from the Tree of Knowledge of Good and Evil, which Adam and Eve were invited by Satan to come and taste. There are two sides to every story, and this picture could not play out more vividly in the first account of human history. We always have a choice. We have a choice because of God's justice and love to go to Him or to go away from Him.

We have a choice to follow, to obey, to listen, to pray, or not.

The choice is ours to make.

Whatever choice we make is followed by consequences. These consequences can be good or bad. Every decision will have repercussions that follow us all of our lives.

You may remember the story of Noah from when you were growing up. This story seems so simple. A guy built a big boat, which then became a zoo when he loaded all the animals on it. It rained for a long time, and therefore the boat began to float on the water, carrying the family and the animals around. The waters subsided, the boat landed, and they all lived happily ever after. This is the account that most children can tell you. Honestly, this is the shallow depth our Bible stories today. We miss the point. Sometimes we forget the ones who were lost during this flood. The reality was death, destruction, devastation. Noah and his family lost loved ones, friends, acquaintances, their home, their way of life, all because God called Noah to go. Going is not often easy or simple. Going requires faith, hope, love, in the midst of situations that feel faithless, hopeless, and loveless. God called Noah to build an ark. The idea of that sounds really cool... God calling someone to build a boat. Can you imagine the depth and length that you would go to try and exactly make a specific item for God? Wanting to put forth your best effort, the tedious attention to detail would become almost mind numbing. You would tune out everything and be fully focused on the task ahead.

That is what Noah did for 120 years. Can you imagine working on a project for that long a boat you are building in the middle of dry land? I imagine if God called me to build a boat in the middle of North Carolina, or Arizona on dry land, I would probably not be considered the smartest person on the block. It would not be dubbed the coolest project to work on. I would definitely get picked on and probably bullied. I imagine that the bullying that happened to Noah and his family would far surpass the unfortunate bullying that happens in our society today. God had Noah worked on this boat for 120 years.

Remember this also was giving the people around Noah the opportunity to listen to God and to "go" to him for 120 years. He was also giving the people an opportunity to change their ways. Then when it is all said and done, we see God following through with His plan and in chapter seven verse one of Genesis, He says, "Go into the ark, you and your whole family, because I have found you righteous in this generation." It took 120 years for God finally to tell Noah to go. It took 120 years of preparation. One hundred and twenty years of family ridicule was endured. For 120 years Noah did not see the end in sight and remained faithful. There were 120 years of opportunities to have doubt, fear, hopelessness. If we broke it down to how we measure time today, imagine, 43,800 days, 1,051,200 hours, 63,072,000 minutes, and 3,784,320,000 seconds. That is a longggggggg time. It is more than our lifetimes. Can you imagine working on one project alone for more time than you will even be given on this earth? That is a reality that is hard for me to grasp.

Have you been faithful to the call to go for 120 years? This brings new meaning to obedience and hope for a brighter tomorrow. Because of Noah, we have a story that continues. Due to his faithfulness, we ultimately get a savior. Through Noah, God gives us a second chance. We still screw up. We still fail. We still walk away from God. However, God relentlessly pursues us in a way that we can never explain or comprehend.

Abraham is told by God to go. Chapter twelve of Genesis recounts the conversation that happens between God and Abraham (who at this time was still Abram). If you haven't read this story, God gives Abram a name change. God declares that out of Abram a great nation will follow. He cries that Abram will be a blessing and that those who bless Abram will be blessed. God even states that everyone will be blessed because of Abram. This is a huge honor for Abram. Prior to this conversation, the Lord had spoken to Abraham in a direct but not as specific declaration. The Lord called Abram to go. "Leave your country, your people and your father's household and go to the land I will show you" (Genesis 12:1). This is a huge step of faith that Abram is called to take.

God is calling Abram to leave his family, his people, and his country. God is calling Abram to a place that is unknown and not revealed to him. What a step of faith. Can you imagine? What a reminder that for the one of the greatest ancestors in the lineage of Christ, there were times when he didn't even know what was going on. There were times when Abram didn't know the next steps or where to turn. All he knew was to have faith and obedience in God's provision and God's sovereignty. Have you ever had those moments where you feel God is moving you to close a door on a relationship, a job, a living situation or maybe even change locations? Do you struggle to peek out into the hall and see if there is another door or window that you can see open, before you have to fully close the door behind you or where you are?

These are the situations I find myself in more often than I want to admit. I have sensed God calling me at different times in my life to be open to His leading, yet I have not been willing. Sound familiar? It is in these small and often scary moments that we search, seek, and often pray the hardest. We look for any light in the darkest of spaces. When we are stuck in the hallways of life, we forget that we are supposed to praise God there, also. Our "hallways" sometimes produce the most authentic worship, the deepest faith and the humble realization that we can't do life alone. There is great awakening in also realizing that we never are alone.

These hallways remind me so much of my school experience. From outside hallways to large tiled walkways, each school varied. Growing up in public school in the South meant a few things. You got out for the slightest sneeze of snow, and people went hog wild and acted as if they had never driven before. You had to worry sometimes about hurricanes, random crazy summer storms that would pop up out of nowhere, and produce the tornados. School systems would even worry about tornados. They would make the students practice if a tornado came to the school. Tornado drills were always really awkward drills. All the students and the teachers were required to pile out into the hallways of the school, or in the center of whatever building they were in, to find the place with the fewest things that could fly and crash on you. This was all in hopes that these areas would provide the most protection. The fetal position was in full effect as you lined the hallways with your head tucked between your knees and your feet against the lockers, and you were required to be silent (which no one told you would be the hardest part).

After you sat there for a few minutes, they would declare an "all clear" and allow your day to go seemingly back to normal. Yet something about this drill sticks out in my mind. You are in an area where you can't see outside to find out if the tornado is coming or not. You must rely on your other instincts-your hearing and smell. Listening to hear that "train" noise or something blowing off, and smelling the air to sense wind, storm or something to change. There is anticipation in moments like this.

We were on a field trip one time on the coast of Florida with my middle school class. Brave teachers thought it would be a good idea to load us on a bus and take us to NASA. They were crazy, but I am glad they did it. Whoever initiated that trip was a very brave soul. We stayed in a hotel where we could see the beach (a wonderful plus I might add). A large storm quickly formed off the coast. Before we really knew what we were doing, we were rushed into the stairwell of the hotel by hotel security. This was the place with the most cement. We sat there quietly because there was a tornado sighting down the shore and we were under a tornado warning. The sense of hearing was piqued by the tornado sirens going off across the city. Knowing there was nothing that we could do and with many other hotel guests, we waited. We hoped that we would be able to go outside and play on the beach some more, because this was seriously cutting into our free time. Remember I was in middle school. Imminent danger to me meant, no free time with life threatening winds. However, we knew at this moment that sitting in the stairwell and being somewhat better protected was a better use of our time.

Every once in a while, the hotel security personnel would pop their heads in the stairwell, making sure we were still okay, and for a brief moment while the door was open, we were able to see outside. The door opened enough for us to see down the hall and look out a window, which showed the dark sky that was stirring on the middle of what had been a sunny afternoon. Eventually the staff came to the steps and said that we had been given an all clear and we could go about our business for the rest of the afternoon. This moment left an imprint on me. I did not know what was going on. A tornado could hit at any moment. This put not just my day, but my life into perspective. We don't know our time of waiting, our time of yearning, any more than we know the moments that we have remaining here on this earth. This can either freak you out or help you find comfort in the One that is solely removed from time, who sees, knows and is all. I hope it does the latter.

We are often in these moments of the hallway with God. There are times we cannot see what is coming in our lives. It could be a tornado, or nothing. It could be the biggest blessing or our biggest fear. We must at this time lean into something other than our senses. We lean into the Holy Spirit and the people around us and they help carry us through this time of the unknown and unseen. They help us "go," even if we are not sure where, what, why or how. Living a life of "what if's" gets you nowhere. However, if you know and trust the One who is in charge of "today" He will take you through it all. Let's return to Joseph and see how he trusted God as he lived out his "what ifs".

Joseph is first mentioned as one of the twelve sons of Jacob in chapter 35 of Genesis. He was one of two children by one of Jacob's wives, Rachel. Later in scripture we find out that Rachel was Jacob's favorite wife. This leads to even more problems initially for Joseph and the battle that would begin between his brothers, who had three other mothers. (This is not your Sunday school version of this story). The lineage of Esau's descendants (another really weird but cool family story) interrupts the story of Jacob. We pick the story of Joseph backup in chapter 37. Joseph is found at seventeen years of age to be Jacob's favorite son. Jacob adorned him with a multicolored robe. This robe and special attention to Joseph does not set well with his brothers. Feeling left out and neglected, Joseph adds salt to the wound as the story continues. Annoyed at the favoritism shown by Jacob, his brothers became bitter. Joseph opens his mouth, telling them of a dream where the fields of grain, and stars which represented each one of the brothers bowed down to Joseph. This is a big mistake, and the brothers at this point have had it with Joseph.

They do not support his dream because it makes them feel unequal, in the eyes of their father. Some could argue that the brothers felt God's view of Joseph was distorted, in that God found favor in Joseph and not in them. Joseph found himself in many seemingly impossible situations that he was often forced into. I am all about supporting the ideas of one another. I love to help make situations which seem impossible become a reality. However, I am human and there are some dreams I humanly don't want to support. I am jealous that I did not dream it or come up with the idea first. Deja vu hits, and I get stuck in this mentality that I thought of it first became mad that I did nothing about it. This goes back to the "idea world" where we sometimes try to live. Not only that, but it just down right makes me mad. What right does anyone have to say that someone can't or should not do something. I find sometimes, that I am the one on the other side being the oppressor and not the one being oppressed.

Life is full of traps, and we can easily get caught in them. We must remain aware of what is going on around us. We must continuously create motive checks on our thoughts, ideas, actions and behaviors. We need to make sure that we are not being an oppressor to others, but a motivator for positive change.

At the next opportunity, the brothers take it upon themselves to do something. Are we often like this with God? God tells us something or reveals something to us about our lives, and we take it to a point. Then we reach our limit of patience, hope, courage. The next sign that we have that could possibly be an out, we take, grabbing with both fists. We act as if this was our plan all along, that God wasn't able to take care of the situation; or even worse He told us to do something but our actions were the antithesis of His nature. Playing God NEVER ends well.

The brothers, despite their better judgment, make a rash decision and sell Joseph. They tear his coat. The brother takes the false information back to their father that Joseph had been killed. This does not earn the father's love for the brothers any more than before; instead it turns Jacob to mourning. The dreams of Joseph look as if they were the only true death in this story. That was not the case. God has a different plan.

Some time passes and Joseph is brought to Egypt. This guy named Potiphar buys Joseph. God blesses Joseph and the works he does in Potiphar's house. After Joseph has served for a time in the home, Potiphar's wife sets Joseph up in hopes that Joseph will break his integrity. Though Joseph is faithful to his integrity and to God, it causes him to flee from this position of power which he had worked hard to obtain. Once he flees and Potiphar talks to his wife, Potiphar is mad and has Joseph placed in prison.

Have you ever felt like this? You have a dream and it is going well and on track; then all of the sudden, the dream is ripped out from under you. It seems hopeless. It seems like all doors are closed, and that God isn't working in the situation however let's keep reading in this passage. Prison is where more of Joseph's glorious story begins to unfold. After spending time in jail, Joseph is placed in charge of all the prisoners enchained with him. This leads to some interesting conversations for Joseph. The dreamer (Joseph)- the one who had this great idea at the beginning of the story is then given by God the opportunity to interpret two other prisoners' dreams. Two different workers of the king, a baker and a cupbearer, are placed in prison with Joseph. These two both have dreams that disturb them. Joseph offers his services of dream interpretation and ultimately interprets that one would work again for pharaoh, and one would be put to death.

We have all seen this happen before. Some dreams work out, and some dreams fall to pieces. There might even be two people with the same dream, and they have drastically different results. What matters is not necessarily the dreams' success or failure, but what you do with that success or failure. If it fails, how are you putting together the pieces to glorify God? If it succeeds, how are you using your success to make it clear that you are thankful to your Creator? Both extremes, as well as the intermediate, are hard to manage.

The story at this point could have taken many different turns. God could have intervened in the life of the baker and saved him. God could have gotten all of them out of prison. Joseph could be left to work out his days in the prison. That could be the ultimate ministry that God called for in his life. This would not have been a bad ministry. It could have left Joseph to impact people over and over again who at one point had made a poor decision. After his counsel, those same people could go on to become a great disciple for Christ. Although this is a great goal and concept, it was not God's plan for Joseph's life.

There are so many times when we have been struck down by one decision or another, that we feel God has left and forsaken us. We have gone somewhere that led us to what seemed a dead end. There are times when we think we have God's plan figured out, and realize that it may not be our first choice, but that we could glorify Him by doing something different. In Hebrews 13, scripture reminds us that He never leaves or forsakes us. Praise the Lord. Joseph works through the decisions that he made and the decisions that were made for him (being thrown in jail). He comes out ready to serve God in whatever way God states or directs.

God uses the dreamer in Joseph, his original characteristic that created the first interpretation that got him in trouble with his brothers. This same characteristic caused the brothers to sell him into slavery. Characteristics are given to us by God with a responsibility to use them for His goodness, and to further His kingdom. This dream defining feature goes on to save Egypt from famine years down the road. God likes to use our defining features when we least expect it. As you continue reading, be thinking about the features that define you. How is God using you in ways that are different from the ones who are around you? You may not see that He is using your defining features now; however, he is training and preparing you for something. God works in mysterious ways, always.

Let me give you an example. I was never good at being quiet in church. No matter how hard I tried and how many pieces of paper that I had to draw on, I never was the greatest at either keeping still or being quiet. My mom and dad will be laughing and nodding their heads when they read this, knowing it is true. It is something that I just did not do well, and still don't. I could listen to the sermon. It could make sense and I could be impacted. I was still always doing something during the message. The constant "sit still" or "be quiet" was in effect at all times. Although I don't remember too many times being disrespectful about it, or at least I tried not to be, I just couldn't do it.

A few years later, off to college and graduate school I went, and somehow by God's grace ended up back at my church being an interim children's minister. I loved this time in my life. Being able to be with the children and teach them about Christ was awesome. I was able to sit in the floor with them and listen to their days at school or play in the nursery with the two-year olds who had just learned "Peek a Boo". My gift, or curse, of not sitting still or always talking, depending on who you talk to, came in very handy. It still comes in handy. I understood the need to not have idle hands, (Proverbs 16:27), and I always found something to do.

The time would come where I would have to pray, or do the announcements or speak in the worship service. This brought my "non" stillness and "non" quietness full circle. Now at this point in time, I was the only one who in those moments was supposed to be speaking. These were the times that, as a child, I would want to speak the most now I could and I did. Those moments justified all the times that I was asked to be quiet or sit still. They all made sense because God was using my gift of being able to move around and talk to glorify Him. Though I am not in that position anymore, I have felt like Joseph not knowing how to use my gifts, but only knowing that they needed to be used. God always finds a way to open a door, or at least a window, if you just pay attention.

Now back to the story, Joseph's interpretation of the cupbearer's (butler's) dream is about to gain the attention of the Pharaoh. The butler was back at work with the Pharaoh, when the Pharaoh himself has a dream that shakes him to the core. This is the prime moment, one in which Joseph cannot control...one which was planned by God to happen. The butler remembers about the interpretation of his own dream by Joseph and how it came true. Then the butler speaks on Joseph's behalf. When we are open and willing to be a vessel for God to use, anything is possible. In Isaiah we see a two-way conversation happening between God and Isaiah. There is this questioning of God of whom to send, and Isaiah steps up to the challenge and declares to God to send him.

"And I heard the voice of the Lord saying, "Whom shall I send, and who will go for us?" Then I said, "Here am I! Send me. He said, Go and tell this people: Be ever hearing but never understanding, be ever seeing but never perceiving." Isaiah 6:8-9.

God then gives Isaiah the words to say in Isaiah 6:9-13. It is amazing to see the follow through that God has with Isaiah. He not only tells him to go, but tells Isaiah what to say. I think this is an important reminder. When we are not eloquent or at a loss for words, God will provide the words or the silence needed in whatever situation we face.

We hear the first part of this verse so often, the common cause for us to be sent and to be used by God. I have seen God work, as we go globally, I am a testament to that. I have also seen people at home here being used, and God working in them while they are here, with so many global implications. There is a mindset that as Americans, we are often exempt from the world and its problems. I often hear some people say that a situation is one country's responsibility to deal with, and we are exempt from anything. Yet there is a reason that we are also dubbed the "melting pot" country. We have people from all over the globe interacting with us, living in our communities, participating in our customs and even fighting for our freedom. So to say this seems a little distant, a little removed, and more condescending than I honestly want to admit. The second part of this scripture is what really makes a difference for me. Once we are sent, we are not just to do whatever we please

Verse nine says that we are supposed to always be hearing, implying that there is always something new to hear. Then it continues that we are never to be understanding the layers in which customs and cultures are formed and created. With intense study and depth, we find that there is always more left to learn and a new leaf to uncover. Then it also states that we should be ever seeing. We should be ever looking to the new opportunities that God gives us each day to impact others. We should look for ways we can help, ways we need to surrender to ourselves and ways that we need to obey God, no matter where we are.

There are times when we think we know the next step and perceive what is going on, only to discover that it was incorrect from the beginning. These two verses, though simple and short, show the beautiful complexity of our God. He can take two mundane things that each of us do every day, seeing and hearing - and turn them into a way to tune into his will and his way. May we forever be sent and open to the sending, but may we also ever be open to the hearing and seeing while we are there.

What we do while we are gone makes a difference in the way we react to situations, especially internationally. Many times it sets the tone for the way people view our customs and culture. What legacy do you want to leave? The butler at the time of Pharaoh's dream had an opportunity to speak for the oppressed, and that is just what he did. There are times when our voices are so far away from the ones who need to hear them. Others have to speak for us. Reminding Pharaoh of his past mistakes (this alone could have landed him back in jail or worse killed), the cup bearer continues to speak of someone whom Pharaoh has never met. Often hearts have to be softened for voices to be heard. Had Pharaoh not had a dream, restored the relationship and job of his cup bearer, the story of Joseph would have ended in jail. I expect Joseph had similar thoughts over the two years that he remained in chains after interpreting the baker's and cupbearer's dreams. We need to be reminded that God so many times in our lives puts a comma where we put a period. After the cup bearer speaks Joseph is summoned by Pharaoh. Joseph is brought from prison and is put to work interpreting the dreams of Pharaoh.

This is not how Joseph had planned his life. He went from being sold to being placed in prison to thinking he had an out at one point working for someone else - but God had a different plan. Do you ever feel this way? Trial after trial, temptation and setback one after another God may be quieter than normal, but He is never away from your side. His plan is out of time, out of our understanding. His spirit is with us to guide, direct, lend us hope in the middle of life's chaos, mess, mud and mire. Just think of the times in your life that it feels as if family or friends have turned on you. Have there been times when you were caught up in something and did not realize how you got there in the first place? It was not your plan to have this job or live in the area that you do. You never thought you would have that addiction and have debt up to your ears. Somehow you have found yourself in these positions.

Unyielding to what is ahead of you, you feel there is something more, but don't know to get there. Life has to be more than what it has been for you and literally you, don't know who, where or how to turn. God is there. Grace is there. Hope, redemption, freedom is there. It will not be easy. Life creates ripples and there will be setbacks along the way. The fight will be worth it.

After interpreting the dream of Pharaoh, Joseph is found with favor and is appointed to be over the land of Egypt during the time of plenty, and a time in famine that had been discovered in Pharaoh's dream. Only at this point in the story do we hear of Joseph's brothers again. When Pharaoh had Joseph interpret his dream, he put Joseph in charge during the famine that he forecasted was to come. This allowed Joseph to be in charge of storing and dispersing the food for the land. The brothers who caused all this trouble are now coming to Joseph for help. God likes to bring things full circle. The brothers and Jacob have been hit hard by the famine, and despite their own efforts, they are left to ask for food from Pharaoh because they do not have enough for their family. Jacob sends ten of the brothers to get grain from Egypt (where Joseph now lives working with Pharaoh). Jacob keeps Benjamin with him. He is not allowed to travel, because this is the only other son of his favorite wife Rachel. He does not want harm to come to Benjamin. As the brothers approach Joseph they are not able to recognize him. Joseph, the person who is about to be their family's redemption, is the person they enslaved so many years ago. After questioning the brothers and their intentions, Joseph sends one of the brother's home to fetch Benjamin, and the others are placed in jail until they both return. This is a harsh punishment for the brothers. Does Joseph want to check their intent? Have the brother's motives changed from when he was thrown into slavery? The brothers still do not realize that they are in the presence of their brother. Joseph is using an interpreter to speak for him. The brothers do not realize that Joseph can understand what they are saying. Reuben, the oldest brother, speaks up at this point. He mentions the turmoil they are currently enduring is because of what they had done to Joseph so many years ago. In Genesis 42:22, Reuben replies, "Didn't I tell you not to sin against the boy? But you wouldn't listen! Now we must give an accounting for his blood." What a great reminder that we always need to be someone else's advocate.

At a time when they think Joseph is dead and no longer has a voice, Reuben becomes a voice for him although not in his greatest hour of need as he should have. This is a reminder that we have opportunities to make differences in the lives of people all the time. It shows us that we can miss out on opportunities to speak on behalf of others. Speaking for someone does not always mean that we will be heard the first time. That should not prevent us from continually trying to speak for what is correct and honorable.

We see this same advocacy in the story of Moses. Moses' sister Miriam is the one who starts the journey of Moses that could have never happen without her quick thinking and wise words.

Exodus 2:1-10

2 Now a man from the house of Levi went and took as his wife a Levite woman. 2 The woman conceived and bore a son, and when she saw that he was a fine child, she hid him three months. 3 When she could hide him no longer, she took for him a basket made of bulrushes and daubed it with bitumen and pitch. She put the child in it and placed it among the reeds by the river bank.4 And his sister stood at a distance to know what would be done to him. (ESV)

The story of Moses begins during a time of much turmoil in the Bible. There was a huge risk the mother took as she attempted to hide her son for three months. When she could no longer hide him properly, her plan had to change. This new plan would seriously change the course of history. The mother was amazingly smart. We see this by the meticulous care she gave her child. She took strategic care to create the basket where she was going to hide Moses. Have you ever thought about how big a basket would have to be to hide a three-month-old? It would take some time and effort to make a basket not only that big, but sturdy enough to hold a baby.

We see that the basket is placed in the reeds near Pharaoh's daughter's washing area. Though I love the depiction of Moses avoiding the alligators and oars of the boat that you see in the Disney depiction of "The Prince of Egypt" I don't believe this depiction would have been correct. The stealth nature that the mother would take to place him quietly in the river without being seen would be astounding. The mother would have even been scared to place him in the water where she did, because it was close to the palace where someone might see her. For under the rule of Pharaoh, all the Hebrew sons born were to be killed. The Hebrew girls were allowed to live. The mother had to risk letting baby Moses go to allow him to grow up, and to have him ultimately come closer.

Now Moses had an older sister, one who seemed to be either wise or risk taking beyond her years. Genesis 2:5-6 *Now the daughter of Pharaoh came down to bathe at the river, while her young women walked beside the river. She saw the basket among the reeds and sent her servant woman, and she took it. 6 When she opened it, she saw the child, and behold, the baby was crying. She took pity on him and said, "This is one of the Hebrews' children."*

She wanted to know what was going to happen to her brother. You have to give the girl some credit for bravery here. As she watched the events unfold, and saw Moses float into Pharaoh's area, I can only imagine her holding her breath to see what words were spoken first. Would they instantly kill him? What would they do? She was at risk as was her family by acknowledging anything to do with the child. If Moses had fallen into the wrong hands, this could have resulted in her and/ or her family's death. This is a big leap into the unknown for the girl in the story.

We can look at the journey that Miriam takes to see what happens next. Her brother, because of her mother's act of bravery and her sister's quick thinking, becomes one of the chosen ones of Israel to come back and save his people from his adopted grandfather, Pharaoh. Miriam offers to Pharaoh's daughter to call a Hebrew nurse for Moses. Exodus 2:7-10 *Then his sister said to Pharaoh's daughter, "Shall I go and call you a nurse from the Hebrew women to nurse the child for you?" 8 And Pharaoh's daughter said to her, "Go." So the girl went and called the child's mother. 9 And Pharaoh's daughter said to her, "Take this child away and nurse him for me, and I will give you your wages." So the woman took the child and nursed him. 10 When the child grew older, she brought him to Pharaoh's daughter, and he became her son. She named him Moses, "Because," she said, "I drew him out of the water." (ESV- Bible Gateway)*

When we go, there is always a risk involved. Always. Are we willing to risk much in hope for a great reward? How big do we often "go" for God? Later in scripture we see several times where Moses "goes" to the people and grows closer to God. Yet at times we all miss opportunities to "go." Are you looking for your next "go" moment?

Joseph was paying attention to what was happening with his brothers, and the emotions that they were going through. Not only was he watching their actions and demeanor, he was listening to what they were saying about his brother, his dad and even himself. We are always being watched. Our lives and our actions make a difference whether we realize it or not. This does not mean that we need to rush into decisions. Sometimes we even make things impossible. We need to think about the consequences, both good and bad, of our actions. When we are given a job by God, we need to pay attention to the little things. It is the little things that we realize later have turned into the big events or circumstances. These little moments matter, and that makes a difference.

Looking further along Moses' career, we see that little turning moments made the biggest impact in his journey. God called him to become the great person of faith that we think of today. God called him to pay attention to a little thing that was out of the ordinary. Moses was called by God to be aware and to be present in his circumstances. There was something about this moment that made it special. The bush that was not being consumed made for something eternal, something significant, something out of the ordinary. This meant that the bush was giving one's attention.

What are the different areas in our lives that God uses to cause us to question whether they are eternal or not? Is God calling you to give your attention to something different? Is He calling you to pay more attention to something you are already involved in? This is where the Holy Spirit comes into play.

Moses took this opportunity to listen and hear what God was asking him to do. He did this by paying attention to the bush. Moses may or may not have understood the risk that was involved initially, but he was willing to try, to be out of his comfort zone and to be curious. There are times when we all miss opportunities to "go" for God.

The excuses are as numerous as the grains of the sand. Are you looking for your next "go" moment? Often we are just looking to make it to the next step in the journey not enjoying the journey itself.

Joseph finds his next "go" moment literally as his brothers are packing up to leave. He gives them silver in their bags. I believe that this act was not out of condemnation, but out of hope that Joseph would begin to take his brothers on a journey of thinking a different way. When they get home, they realize this mistake and again fell judged by God and the things that they did to their brother. Joseph uses the tool of silver to bring up a memory that has been pushed away. He brings it up so the brothers can have another chance to make amends.

They realize later that they need to go back and ask Joseph for more grain. So off they go. The brothers know the questions that Joseph asked previously. They warn their father and ask Jacob to take Benjamin with them. The family then doubles the amount of silver to take back, so they will not get thrown into jail. They do not want any harm to come to them. Many times God uses scripture like this to propel us into ministry in ways we never thought possible. Though there are fears that we must push aside if we act in obedience to God and His word, He is always faithful.

Check out Heath's story.

I met a student from Malaysia in graduate school, and over the next few months God placed on our hearts and a few others to lead a college conference in Malaysia. During our time there we also had the opportunity to lead worship at various churches. It was my first international trip and it was only by the grace of God that He drew the right people together. We took our love for God and worship to students on the other side of the world. I was truly blessed because I got to see followers of Christ live out their faith in a Muslim country.

This pastor had started a church in Malaysia, but felt God leading him to start churches throughout the jungles as well. As he was carrying the gospel to other areas of Malaysia many people came to know Christ and churches began to start; some two hours from where he lived. The news of him began to spread and the Malaysian government became aware of what he was doing which was a problem since it is a Muslim country. The government officials told him that he needed to stop what he was doing or he would be put in jail. This didn't stop the pastor because he knew that God had called him to do this. One day he was put in jail because he would not adhere to the commands of the government. Just like Joseph in Egypt, he used the opportunity in jail to make much of Christ so he began to preach to his fellow inmates. Many of the inmates came to Christ because God was being glorified even through this.

The pastor would serve his jail time and be released, but it didn't stop him from going back to where he left off. He kept being put in jail and each time more and more inmates came to Christ. So many inmates were coming to Christ that they quit putting him in jail. They even began to have him come and be a chaplain because they could see the great impact he had on the inmates and their change since becoming followers of Christ.

As a Christian in America I can freely worship God and go out into my community and share my faith without the consequences of doing so. How much more should I live a life worthy of the gospel locally because God puts me in the path of people on a daily basis that are separated from God. The stories I heard and the trip I was a part of gave me the passion to return home and live intentionally. The community I live in is the mission field that God has called me to and I should be passionate about making an impact for Christ.

Christianity was not something that they had added onto their lives; it was their life. That trip gave me a better understanding of how I should live my life everyday as a follower of Christ. A verse 1 Thessalonians 2:8 comes to mind and it says, "We cared so much for you that we were pleased to share with you not only the gospel of God but also our own lives, because you had become dear to us." It means we should live our lives intentionally meeting needs and investing in others that are separated from Christ. As we sacrifice of our time and begin to build relationships with people it gives us the opportunity to meet their spiritual need as well. It means more than going on a mission trip when they occur. It means taking the extra step and understanding that your mission field is wherever God has you right now. That means your family, your work, your friends and your neighborhood.

When I graduated, I was given the opportunity to serve as the missions director at my home church and it was a great way to share what God had put on my heart and to show others what it really means to live our lives on mission for Him every day. To this day I am still serving in that position and God has given our church the opportunity to partner with a local school. We are meeting the physical needs of students through a food ministry so each week they have something to eat over the weekend. We have had the opportunity to build relationships with the teachers and staff there and along the way we have had some of them come to know Christ as their Lord and Savior. I pray that God keeps molding me into who He wants me to be as I grow in my faith and try to lead others in a way that leads us all to make an impact for Christ.[5]

Now back to Joseph and his brothers. The brothers gain new perspective.

They hope.

They prepare.

They ponder.

Other stories throughout the Old and New Testament show us a perspective change. Daniel and the lion's den, Noah and the building of the ark, Abraham, Ruth, Paul each in their own right have perspective changes.

Zacchaeus gains a new perspective. Literally, emotionally, and physically, his outlook shifts. In Luke 19 we see the story of Zacchaeus. He was a small man, and he could not see Jesus over the crowd that was in front of him. Wanting to see what Jesus looked like, he took the opportunity to be different from the crowd who surrounded him. I imagine that he was not the only one in the crowd that day that could not see Jesus come into town. Zacchaeus was creative in using his resources. I love what he decided to do about it. It got him in the Bible for eternity. By simply climbing a tree, he was able to see something different from anyone else. He positioned himself in a place where Jesus could move and work in his life. This was not Zacchaeus' original intent. He was just looking for a full

---

[5] Heath Stone.

vision of what was happening. Jesus could directly call on him to yield his previous life and change his ways.

Have you ever felt that way? There are times where we are surrounded by chaos and we lose sight of what matters. Little things get in our way, and we can't understand why we are in a rut. However, by positioning ourselves in a different manner and use our creative ability, things change. We are able to see how amazingly wonderfully God can work in and through situations, circumstances, people and places. Zacchaeus went somewhere. He had initiative. By taking this initiative, Zacchaeus gained new perspective of the situation at hand. He was given a new way of looking at the world and the people around him, and in turn, the world and the people around him looked differently at Zacchaeus. He was noticed, he was invited and he was transformed by this new perspective.

Many times on mission trips we are willing to stop the schedules, the phones, and the technology of our previous lives if only for a weekend or week. We take the time out to hope that we can gain a different perspective on life. Many times we even do things on mission trips that are not normal in our daily lives. Things such as diving into the word more, getting out of our comfort zone or speaking to strangers are often added to our schedule.

All the missions I have experienced have changed my perspective. I hope it is the same for you. Mission trips are just like the tree in the story of Zacchaeus. The trips give us a creative outlet to use for God's glory if we choose. They put us in a special place and open our eyes to see what God is doing, if we are lucky enough to pay attention. We, like Zacchaeus, are often called down from the tree by God to experience and walk and learn from him. This happens through our perspective change in and by HIs coming and meeting us where we are.

For every positive, there is often a negative. The negative part of this story is that many people are just like the heretics who say we are too rich or too stingy, or why don't we do something closer to home instead of spending money to go internationally. Local missions are wonderful. Don't get me wrong. I believe in them as much as I do international missions. I believe that everyone should experience at least one international or completely different culture (including language) trip in life. Though these cultural differences can be found in small pockets of our United States melting pot, I believe the best effect is international. This should occur if for no other reason than to get people out of their comfort zones.

The more I go internationally, the more I am fueled by the need that I see all around me locally. I see resources that we have as Americans that are not being used. Other resources are being misused. It takes time as we attempt to talk about changes and appropriation of resources. Yet many times we do not have any action beyond our words. This leads me to get angry, bitter or both, sometimes even at myself for my misuse of everything.

If we just look at the corporate structure of America, we see consistently that we meet to talk about when our next meeting is to occur. Why can't we just meet? Why can't we get things accomplished, meet the needs, discover others, and plan while working forward? Yes, it takes time to plan, but wouldn't it be worth it? The "going away" a little further brings into focus what is right in front of us all the time. This is why so many companies, churches, small groups, and families invest millions of dollars collectively to go on retreats. They take time to get away from the normal distractions to focus on the progress that is to come for the next weeks, months or years.

This pause in their schedule allows them to plan, prepare, question and focus on a unified vision. It gives them perspective on where they have come from, leading them to a vision of their future. This impacts our relationships. The ties that bind us are strengthened when we take away society's distractions. We focus on fixing issues, mending relationships and repairing bridges. We question how we can go back to hurt relationships in the past and say will you forgive me of my past and join me in my future? If we follow through with this, how much better would life look as we became unified for a common cause without the chaos? How does your perspective and your distractions make a difference and change your reality and concept? Do you need a retreat from social media, email, phone signal, co-workers? At different points in our lives these retreats are needed for each of us. The excuses for not taking one are the reason why an estimated 577,212,000 vacation days end up not being used at the end of the year, according to an Expedia.com survey. An estimated 67% of Americans still stay connected and check their email or voicemails while they are away.[6] I have one thing to say. Turn your phone off! We got away without a phone or email for thousands of years- you can handle a week. Now go!!!

We see in scripture people being called to go for the name of Christ. How does it impact us today? Is this something that does not need to continue? Or, is it something that we need to be more passionate about than ever before? There is a wonderful quote from John Piper describing God's pursuit of us.

"God is pursuing with omnipotent passion a worldwide purpose of gathering joyful worshipers for Himself from every tribe and tongue and people and nation. He has an inexhaustible enthusiasm for the supremacy of His name among the nations. Therefore, let us bring our affections into line with His, and, for the sake of His name, let us renounce the quest for worldly comforts and join His global purpose."[7]

I love the language that Piper uses and his imagery. Our God is an omnipotent passionate God. How amazing is the realization that God is passionate for us? He is able to do more than we can ever think or imagine. God, great, glorious, perfect, wonderful God, wants to participate with us and our lives on a consistent basis. This concept blows my mind. God as big and majestic as He is, wants and yearns to participate in our lives.

We see in the New Testament when God calls us through Acts to go to the ends of the earth, but let us start with Jerusalem.

> *"But you will receive power when the Holy Spirit comes on you; and you will be my witnesses in Jerusalem and in all Judea and Samaria and to the ends of the earth." Acts 1:8*

---

[6] (2013 Vacation Deprivation Study, 1).
[7] (John Piper).

People who recognize the work of the Lord continuously in their lives often try to tell others about their experiences. They do this in a myriad of ways, often speaking truth in love, or showing love through their actions. They become witnesses to others where they are.

Jerusalem was the center of Christianity at the time. Everything grew out of Jerusalem. Luke, the writer of Acts, describes the circles of influence that the power and the Holy Spirit should have in our lives. Just like the central hub that Jerusalem was to Christianity, we each have "hubs" of our own. The first circle depicts those immediately around us, in our homes in our families. How we act, speak and impact those closest to us makes the most difference. The biggest impact we have is on the ones we care for and who care for us the most.

The next circle moves further out to Judea. This relates to the ones who are neighbors. This impacts those co-workers we may or may not talk to, the soccer moms, and swimming dads that you see with your children at sports. These are the ones who are your acquaintances. Maybe you even having their number in your phone and will say hello to them. There is little to no depth to the conversations with this group. People in this category are those in your gym class, in your school, your doctors, or friends who work at the grocery store or pharmacy.

The circle spreads even wider to Samaria. Those who are not like us and not in our relational circles belong here. This includes those we have to be intentional about in reaching out and visiting. People within this sphere are not to be ostracized, but reached, impacted and loved, just like the innermost circle.

We see one final circle. This is more closely defined as infinity, and includes all people from all corners of the world. We are called to make these areas aware of the power and presence of God. To influence each of these circles requires a bunch of work. We have a job that is intentionally set before us.

Our circles, how we relate and approach each person, matters. How we interact with and make changes impacts other people. If you have ever seen the movie "Pocahontas", you, maybe like me, found the "Grandmother Willow" willow tree to be slightly creepy as a little child. A talking tree? I didn't understand. The more I think about this reference, the clearer I see that I hear nature talking to me all the time. The rivers, the wind, the water, all represent something different to me about God and His character. Despite the creepy nature of the tree talking, Grandmother Willow makes a good point. Talking to Pocahontas she explains that whenever you throw a rock into a stream, it makes ripples. Good bad or otherwise, the water around where you throw in the rock is displaced. Other water has to move over or out of its way. This creates ripples in the surface of the water.

There is beauty in the ripples. The further out the ripples go, the smaller their effect and change in the water surface. The first ripple closest to the disturbance has the most impact. The last ripple is a faint whisper fading into the unknown. This can apply to our lives. The ones that we affect the most are the ones who are the closest to us. Friends and family we cherish are often brought up or down depending on our actions and responses to situations. However, the acquaintances that we have are not impacted as much. They typically go on with their lives as if nothing happened, other than a small disturbance in the force. This is the present day ripple effect. When we do missions, especially international missions, this present day ripple gets inverted.

Going away closer allows each one of us to be witnesses to the ends of the earth and create ripples that originate in that country instead of faint whispers heard from across oceans. This is why our international travel needs to be so covered in prayer and thoughtful obedience to Christ. Without paying attention to the signs the Holy Spirit gives us, we could do catastrophic damage by creating ripples of ill intent. Ill intent ripples are so much harder to change than the faint whisper.

While on the mission fields, we meet and talk with new friends who become family. For that week, they are closer to us than anyone else. People like these are the ones we impact and love. We share God with them, giving them the largest wave of hope and eternity that they could ever receive. How we invest in prayer and obedience to

God prior to the trip, sets up our potential investment during the trip. Then and only then do we see the immeasurable goodness and joy that comes from setting up ripples of hope, joy, peace and love, in places that are not used to it. God uses each area or discipline that we are a part of to make a difference. It is our responsibility that we make good use of the resources that He has given us. It is stated in Luke 12:48, "To much is given much is required". We are then charged to become positive witnesses for His people and to bring the kingdom closer.

Joseph's life is a great story of redemption, describing the reality that our timing, God's timing and often the world's timing, are hardly ever on the same page. This is not a bad thing, but it's just a realization that when things don't initially go our way, we shouldn't give up. We should not lose hope. We should not stop fighting. God is in the midst of it all, when we can't see, when we don't look and when we know what is right ahead. The family of Joseph is then reunited after a much anticipated time apart. The process is what we find so rewarding. In obedience Joseph followed God as he went away and as he came closer.

One of my favorite songs is called "Break Every Chain" by Tasha Cobbs. This is a very simple and repetitive song that reminds me over and over the majesty and awe of the God that I serve. The song begins by stating "There is power in the name of Jesus." This power is something that I cannot understand. This power is something beyond my imagination bigger than all the "World's Strongest Man" competitions and the World Wrestling Federation that you see on television. Though these shows, display great strength, they are not capable of infinite power. It is amazing to think that America is often compared to the lives and personalities that are shown on WWF and MTV (Music Television). These are two channels that I am not proud are shown on American television.

I found it jaw-dropping while traveling into a few remote villages to see the depravity of their living conditions. Villagers may not have a bed, or have a bed that is tightened by ropes that hold sheets that are layered on top. They might have a single electricity line if they have one at all and maybe one electrical outlet in their home. Of the countries I have visited, if people were fortunate enough to have electricity, they most likely had a television on a dirt floor. Two of the few channels that they would get, hosted MTV and WWF. This became the reality in which their view of the United States and its residents was framed. It was not a depiction I could easily change. Showing an unrealistic amount of power and presence, these shows took away the personal nature of who we have the potential to be as a society. Luckily, there are more channels now available for local television and news that represent a slightly better depiction of the United States.

Jesus' power is of a different nature, supernatural. It has the ability to break not just a chain but "every" chain. Our chains come in so many different forms, yet Jesus and His power have the ability to come through those hindrances and mend the broken, heal the sick and make the blind see. It displays the might, strength and glory of a man who walked on water and was raised from the dead. The amazing thing is that we, through the amazing nature of God somehow get to see and take part in this power.

Some days I am not sure why God allowed this. Every day, however, I am glad that He allows us to work and move on His behalf. It is through working and witnessing His work that we can share in some glorious experiences. This power is called the Holy Spirit, and we see it manifested on Jesus during his baptism as it descended on him in the form of a dove. (Matthew 3:16-17). Later in Matthew we hear Jesus talking about our mission and the call in our lives. We have this duty within us to make disciples.

"Go therefore and make disciples of all nations, baptizing them in the name of the Father and of the Son and of the Holy Spirit," Matthew 28:19

If you have ever been a part of a baptism service, it is awesome. There is this amazing stillness and anticipation that infiltrates the room or the area where the baptism occurs. I have been blessed to see many baptisms of friends and family. Each baptism experience is different from the previous one. The place from which the person comes tells a different story and sings a different song. There is something supernatural that makes these moments truly memorable. Each time I witness these events, I thank God and the Holy Spirit for working in the lives of others. I am grateful that He allows us to be witnesses to the greatest moment in their lives.

Baptisms come in different varieties. I have been a part of baptisms that are very quiet. Some have had very few people present and the Spirit was in the place, moving in the moment. There are other times when baptisms take place fully in front of a crowd or at the front of the service. At those the is spirit present. I have witnessed river, lake, ocean, pool and baptistry baptisms. The water has been freezing at some, and at others it felt like a sauna.

It is the symbolic dying to ourselves and raising life to Christ that is amazing. What matters during this moment is not the circumstance and scenery that surrounds the person being baptized. What matters is the spiritual readiness of the person to die to their old life and live a life that will glorify God through word and deed. This is where the profession of faith is so important. It is through the story that the believer is able to share with others that a difference is made.

The Matthew 28 verse is very special to me and the mission of the church, and is the main reason that we are called to share our stories with other people. Not only are we called to bring others to faith to the point they are denying themselves and following Jesus; we are to make disciples. If you look at this discipleship process within scripture, it is not one that is developed from being in someone's life for a brief amount of time. It is important to realize that this transformation is something that is created over a long period of time. As you grow and walk together with each other in ministry and in life, you and others are molded and changed.

There are many churches that are currently focused on the "life group", "small group" or "community group" model. I think this model is displayed within the heart of this verse. We need to grow together as believers, learning and listening and holding each other accountable. Then we are developing a discipleship model within our space without setting a list of rules or steps that have to be followed. We are setting and understanding an example that we are to be disciple makers. This is needed wherever we are and whichever stage of life we find ourselves. What I think that we often miss out on is the true concept of baptism.

People can become great at making friends and walking with them in life. Somehow we often drop the ball on baptizing them and leading them to do the same for others. We get so set in our ways that this (albeit, often awkward) conversation about baptism and discipling sometimes gets thrown to the wayside. We become focused more on the discipling than on the baptizing, for them to do the same. How can this process of discipling lead straight into the process of baptizing? I had the joy of watching one of my life group ladies being baptized recently at church with her son. Her story is one of power.

When I was asked to write down my testimony, I thought two things. One, it's a long story, and two, it didn't begin with me. It began with my mother. As a child she grew up Roman Catholic in Costa Rica. It was the way of life for our family there. She went to a Catholic school, and when she wasn't learning from the nuns, she would be at church with her family. But like all kids, you question what you are made to do. But instead of getting the explanations, she was told that children are seen and not heard and that she must do what she was told. So that did not strengthen her foundation with her religion. She was introduced to another religion when she met my dad's mother. She was a Jehovah's Witness- a complete 180. They encouraged questions and talk about the work of Jehovah.

When she came to the United States, she continued her practice. I grew up in the Kingdom Halls. I had fun but now, like my mother. I had questions about my religion. My mother told me once that her old religion was forced upon her and it made her resent the church. She wanted us to have the free will to find our god our way, but still encouraged that through God all things are possible. Why couldn't we celebrate Christmas? Because that's not when Christ was born. Why don't we celebrate Easter? Because we don't celebrate Jesus's death. Why can't I celebrate my birthday? Because John the Baptist's head was cut off and presented on a platter so it represents a birthday cake.

Man, these were hard for a kid at Christmas parties. I would sit in the hallway and watch my class exchange presents and have fun without me. The fact that I couldn't celebrate my birthday was hard knowing I am here on earth another year alive and well was even harder especially since I loved birthday cake. As we grew up, my mother wasn't an acting Jehovah's Witness after a while, so we did celebrate Christmas and birthdays, but prayed to Jehovah. This was kinda like Catholics not really being Catholics until Easter and Christmas. So my heart wasn't in love with the church. I still believe in something bigger and holy. I tried being a Catholic, going back to my mother's roots, but I felt like no one explained anything, and there was so much to remember. I felt like an animated wound doll: "sit, kneel, stand, kneel raise hands," say these specific phrases and do the cross and amen. It felt automated to me, but I knew God was with me.

At times I felt His presence, but I didn't know where exactly to find Him. I would talk to Him time and again. "Hey God, It's me again: How you doing? Well you know what I am doing. If you would help me, I would never change," I remember someone in book camp told me that times would get tough, but on those hot days when I feel God, through the cool breeze He would remind me He's with me and I could do it. That helped me through a lot in my life. My best friends invited me to their church one day. It was both non-denominational and Christian followers. It opened up my eyes. I liked the praise and worship. The message was great. The pastor would bring his own personal stories into the message. He made it relatable. I felt like I was in the right path; that I belonged among them. They were speaking my language.

During my discovery, my mother was going through a divorce. She called me up Sunday afternoon crying. She couldn't deal with the separation. She didn't want to continue on. This woman who was my rock and the strongest person I know completely fell apart. I left work to find her almost inconsolable. It was breaking my heart. The first thing that came to mind was take her to church. She agreed. It was around 5:30 pm on Sunday and I was driving to the church I have been attending, not knowing if it was open. As I drove through town, I passed many churches and they were closed. I started feeling defeated, praying to God "Please be open, please let someone be there".

I mean I talked my distraught mother out of the comfort of her home to a church she has never been to. I kept driving. When we pulled up, I didn't see any cars in the parking lot, but still I did not turn around. I parked. I told my mom to sit still, I'm going to get some help, and walked up to the entrance chanting "Please let someone be there," please God, please. As I approached the doors, someone was standing there holding the door opened for me! It was if they were welcoming me inside. When I came in the guy asked how could he help. I just burst into tears. I felt relief. I said my mom needed to talk to someone. One of the pastors' wives was there. We sat in a room for two hours- me, my mom, my sister. the pastor's wife and another lady who has been through a difficult divorce also. At first you could tell my mom was hesitant. I mean, she didn't know anything about this religion and this church. During these two hours, through many tears and boxes of Kleenex, I watched my mom's face go from despair, and uncertainty to relief and so many other emotions- but what amazed me was after those two hours, she was smiling. I saw a light in her eyes again and faith restored and renewed as a Christian. Another 180 degrees. They were talking about all the church has to offer. During that night, they were having a teen night. My sister went and got baptized that night.

I saw God work through my mom and sister that day. K-Love was preset on my mom's phone, car, computer, everywhere. We went to church twice a week. Though this I still felt like I was missing something, but I knew I was on the correct path, since God saved my mom and sister.

When I moved I was worried that I wouldn't find a church similar to mine and that I would be lost again. I was getting this slow burn, like when you are fanning the flames in a fire to make it catch and grow. My son's father told me to check out The Cove Church. Like all new things, I was scared. I walked in and i Like praise and worship and then David Porter led us to prayer. So far, so good.

Then a screen came down and Mike Madding was preaching about Koinonia. The friendships we make, the concept of community and the teachings to love, like Jesus. I knew I was home. These were the questions and uncertainties that I have been wrestling with for the longest. Don't discriminate, don't judge, love everyone equally. Love like Jesus did. He didn't turn away from the sinner; he preached God's word. He showed that God was love and kindness. Then that week they mentioned Cove 101 to give the breakdown of what the church is about, and I absolutely love the core values, because those are the values I was looking for in a church. On February 8th, the sermon was about love. This whole time I felt the fire catch, getting warmer and warmer. When they said God doesn't love us back, He loves us first, I was on fire for God. That was the day everything became clear. A peace came over me and I decided that day to get baptized. My son and I became involved in the church, serving on teams. My son attended student ministries and a great change came over him, also. I told him of my plans on getting baptized and asked if he thought about it and understood of taking that step. On March 22nd we both were baptized. I looked forward to every Sunday to see what new things or word I was going to learn from God.

So you see, it didn't start with me. It was moved through my life and people closest to me to take me on the path where I am today. Like a slow moving fire, I caught the love of God and my church and have the eternal Holy Spirit moving within me and I am thankful every day that the fire will be distinguished.

I think that when this discipleship is completed correctly and effectively, progression and deepening of faith are fruits of that labor. I have also seen great strides in creating this bridge occur when mission trips are the next step in the believers' walk.

Most mission trips are not short on the meetings and fundraiser events that precede the actual trip. The time the team plans together for the trip often supersedes the time in which they are on the ground. This is not a complaint, but often a reality check. As you sign up for a mission trip, are you willing to put the time and effort here on the ground to prepare for your trip? What are we doing within the meetings that make so much difference when we go to the nations (literally)? I think it is what is not on the agenda during those meetings that really makes the most difference. You are in meetings with the people that you will experience life with in a different way, encountering moments that are often out of our comfort zone or even languages barriers. Many times the people that are in the room for the missions meeting are not people that you have met or ever interacted with before. Therefore, there is a need to learn and understand the dynamics of the group.

Sometimes learning the dynamics of the group is created out of ridiculous ice-breaker games, albeit awkward and annoying at points. The little stories can break the biggest pieces of ice. These meetings foster the conversation to be open about the baptizing moments, the Holy Spirit-filled, God-centered, life "stand stilling", mind and heart altering moments. This is where we find it. When we find God, we then see the need for baptism. Finally, we feel and understand the vast reality that so many are lost. It is our responsibility to help them grow if they allow us, and our lives can be lighthouses for Christ. The hope is that one will be brought to the reality of baptism and its importance. What is good for Jesus, is good for me.

May we get to experience the joy that comes from being baptized. Even more, may we experience the joy that comes from being blessed to baptize another. In that brief moment you see the same thing God sees. You are reaching the same person God is cleansing from "I once was blind, dirty, deprived, void, hopeless, "to" I now see, am redeemed, fulfilled, clean, made new, whole."

It is so amazing to think that we share a power with Jesus. That is just a crazy concept and a story for another day. We will be witnesses of this power to others. To be witnesses of something requires you to see something. The literal definition according to Webster is "evidence or proof." How is it that an all-powerful supernatural, ever present omniscient God, allows us not only to see the Holy Spirit (power) but allows it to come upon us as individuals? We can be witnesses only because we have seen the Spirit living and active. It is sharper than any two edged swords, Hebrews 4:12. Amazing things happen when this active spirit works in someone's life or maybe even our own. The Bible expands on this concept of witnessing. There is something more that makes this witnessing different from other times and places, for we are not just to be witnesses of a single event or action, but we are supposed to be active witnesses.

Scripture moves from this idea of witnessing to an active mentality. There is an understanding that we are supposed to be more active about our faith than just being witnesses. We see this come alive in scriptures such as 1 Chronicles 16:24, Matthew 24:14 and Isaiah 52:7. There are many other scriptures that depict the active nature of the gospel. I feel these three are wonderful examples of how God calls us to go both globally and locally.

"Declare his glory among the nations, his marvelous works among all the peoples!"

-1 Chronicles 16:24

How are we to declare what God has done for us if we do not realize what He has done and is doing in our lives? If we are not in the midst of His people to be able to be salt and light to them when they need it, how is God declared? Both are questions that at times are hard to answer. There are times when we are not paying attention to what God is doing. We lose track of how He is working. As this happens we lose focus of the real reason that we are here on this earth. To know God and to make Him known is our purpose. We forget that our obedience to God is shown not only through our faith, but also in our word and deeds. In John Fuder's, "A Heart for the City," he brings this concept to light beautifully.

"Many people don't reject Christianity or the church; they see it as irrelevant. Since being a servant is so contrary to the self-centered. control-obsessed ways of the world, it gives us credibility that we can't have any other way. Instead of being a mirror of the world we become a miracle to the world." [8]

I don't know about you, but the sound of being a miracle to the world stirs a hope and passion within me. As Christians, we have a responsibility to share with others. We have the knowledge of the true miracle. The fact is that God is not in time and space. Things that Christ did in the scriptures are still living and relevant today. This makes our story, our baptism, our declaration more necessary and needed now. Our voices are needed now more than ever before to be light in this dark world. Scripture has the uncanny ability to be relevant in any context. Does God speak specifically to every current context in the scriptures and offer direct advice? No. He offers wise counsel over and over again, warning against times and places which

---

[8] (Fuder, 180).

may take away from Christ being the center and that can and will always be valid.

> *And this gospel of the kingdom will be proclaimed throughout the whole world as a testimony to all nations, and then the end will come."* Matthew 24:14

How will the gospel be preached if the ones who know it do not go to the places that need to hear it? In this passage we see Matthew proclaiming that there is a need for the gospel to be preached to the whole world because it is necessary. This necessity comes out of the end of the verse "then the end will come". If we are called to tell others about the gospel, *then* we will be able to see the fruits of our labor in the end times. There are so many statements similar to this in the scriptures. If you do this, *then* something will happen. These passages should bring us a reminder that God is true to His word and His past actions guarantee future results. You may have missed that. God's past actions "guarantee" future results. Not maybe or might, but results *will* happen. When we are reading scripture, there is a tendency to focus on the beginning and the end of verses. We want to know what happened and how things ended. The middle part of this passage, as well as the middle of many other passages, often gets overlooked.

If we take a moment and look back at Matthew 24:14 we are to go and share the gospel with the whole world. This happens for two reasons. It will bring the end of times and it will also be a testimony to the nations. I think this second part is very important to notice. A testimony is a conversation or action that points to proof of, or in something. By showing other nations who we believe in, we are sharing our story. There is the ability to partake in our testimony, and share in our hope. If we did not share that would be counterintuitive to the gospel and the calling placed on our lives. So many times I have heard of people saying, "well that is not my calling," or "I will let other people do that," and then they don't even put action behind their words locally. This frustrates me sometimes when I, myself, am the one who is choosing not to act. There is a responsibility that comes with acting that is different from just being passive and not being a voice to those around us.

"How beautiful upon the mountains are the feet of him who brings good news, who publishes peace, who brings good news of happiness, who publishes salvation, who says to Zion, "Your God reigns." Isaiah 52:7

You have heard the stories about everyone's grandparents walking uphill both ways in the snow with no shoes to get to school. Though this may or may not be true on a consistent basis, I think the analogy to this verse is worth comparison. There are times in our Christian walk when no matter where we turn, it seems as if we have an uphill battle to climb and the valley is just not able to provide us with the support or growth that we need. We see in Isaiah that on the mountains we are beautiful when we bring the Good News to others. It is hard not to be happy when you are sharing good news with others. If you are not happy then they will question the happiness of the story that you are sharing. It is a catch 22. There are times when we have to make the walk happen to get to the mountain to see the glories that God will show us and bring happiness to others. This is the "mountain top experience." This is also referred to as the mission trip high. When we travel it is a great reminder of perspective and change that is possible when interact with other countries and cultures. We have to also be mindful of this experience. We need to realize there will also be times we find ourselves in the valley lacking vision and discernment.

All of this boils down to faith and works. James over and over again stresses that faith without works is dead and that is basically my same emphasis. What is it if we speak but have no action, if our words are not backed up by what we do? We are missing the mark and making a huge mistake. In James, we see him mention that some will often say that one person has faith and another person has deeds. God did not create us to be compartmentalized. In James 2:26, "As the body without the spirit is dead, so faith without deeds is dead." We are created to act on the passion that God gives us, in obedience with His word and his will, not one without the other but both. Both is often a hard thing to come by, but also to act on. How can we live in a way that our actions back our words and vice versa? I find myself caught in this catch 22 where there are things that I am passionate about, but which are not backed with what I do. There are things that I do and I do not explain the reason why I do them and how God is motivating me to move in a certain way or direction.

This impacts how we "Go" "Away" and bring people "Closer" to God. During these times we see that if we are not meeting the immediate need, it is hard to get through to meet the spiritual need. During this time is when we discover the hard decisions between giving people handouts, versus a hand up and teaching them to fish instead of giving them fish. These empowering processes often take longer amounts of time than just giving people what they need for the moment. They also last longer and create a pathway to betterment and self-sustaining behaviors that make a difference long term. Matthew 5:16 states "In the same way, let your light shine before others, so that they may see your good works and give glory to your father who is in heaven."

How is the light of your actions going to shine locally, regionally, and globally?

How are they going to make a difference in the lives of the people around you?

How is your light shining through your faith, and deeds?

Away

How does it bring back a new perspective to meet the needs of the people who were around you in the first place?

It all started when I was little. There always was a passion to see new things and to experience things that others experienced. I was amazed by pictures of places and new sights and sounds. The food of places did not intrigue me until recent years. I loved looking in the National Geographic that my grandfather would receive in the mail. I would be seeing the elephants and flipping the pages to see the new pictures of all the different cultures that are all around the world. Some of these copies are still at my parents' house today. As I open one the smell of each page reminds my granddaddy and I sitting and reading these page by page. I would sit and dream of the world, what it was like, and what it could be. Then the questions would then flood my head, even at a young age, would I ever see an elephant in its natural habitat? Would I ever go to all the continents?

I don't think he nor I knew but even at this young age the bucket list of my life was beginning. There were so many pictures on these pages that I wanted to witness in person. Things I wanted to see, smell feel and taste. This was then spurred on by the Kratz's brothers (Animal Planet), and other shows that impacted my life. My love of nature set me on a science nerd path. Even though I didn't end up with this major in college provided me with a Biology minor and fascinations to things that other people find boring and mundane. There also is this slight tree hugger in me that hates to waste water and loves to recycle. I even find planting things refreshing. These places created a vision in my mind of the endless possibilities that were before me.

I hated geography growing up. It seemed distant and unimportant. Not only was it just a bunch of different places on a map that I had to memorize for a test and know all the capitals. The only fun portion of geography was that in 7th grade in Mr. Keaton's class I was allowed to color the countries different colors to help memorize each country and the capital. Now, with context, I find the closeness of places to be amazing to see the differences that even ten minutes down the road can make, culturally socioeconomically, and religiously.

Being in year round school when I was little created for some amazing opportunities. This was due to the fact that school schedule was different than the general public, so rates were cheaper. When I was lucky enough to have a break and it would allow for us to go to places. My family along with another family was able to travel to different places in the United States for cheaper rates because it was not the peak season of travel. I remember my first flight and I thought I was going to puke, die, or both at the same time. Thank goodness there was enough faith to get on the plane the first and second time, making my traveling experience better with each flight. After so many flights that I now can't count, I am exceptionally grateful to have semi made it over a hump that I thought would end my travel. Though I still have an issue with sitting still and keeping quiet while on the plane I can constantly continue to work on that.

Family trips were great, new sights and sounds, a souvenir key chain and as many pictures as my parents would let me take on their "film" camera (remember those) and develop. I remember one time going to Wal-Mart after traveling and dropping in eight rolls of film that I had to wait for to send off in the mail. I was too cheap for them to develop it that day. It used to be seven to ten dollars per roll to develop. To get the filmed processed the wait was up to two weeks. if you had panoramic pictures, you would be paying more than that per roll. Little things like this, rotary phones, Gameboys, Polly Pockets, and other concepts kids miss out on these days. Yes, I am that 90's kid with a candy cane colored record player that still runs. Thank you very much.

However, something else was hidden within me. Something that began to come about my junior year in high school. Maybe it was because of the National Geographic, or geography that this evolution was started. Though these travels were great, it was so much fun to see how the places came to life. Once I was able to walk where others had walked my eyes began to be opened more than ever before. Yet, there was something missing from these trips. Something that would bring more out in places than I ever thought possible. Missions, and my passion to see people be reached and walk with God.

Belize 1.0

Doing things with God rather than for God draws us closer to him.

- Donald Miller.

"The command has been to 'go,' but we have stayed — in body, gifts, prayer and influence. He has asked us to be witnesses unto the uttermost parts of the earth ... but 99% of Christians have kept puttering around in the homeland."

— Robert Savage, Latin American Mission

On one normal Sunday, my church announced per usual that they were going on a mission trip. This year it was somewhere they had never been before. Though not the first international mission trip that our church had taken, this was the first one that seemed interesting to me. I had not attended the two that they went on previously. However, something was different about this trip. Something was calling my name to this place. The trip was to Belize, Central America, and at that time my knowledge of geography was exceptionally limited (remember I still hated it, and it had no context). Though it is still limited now, it is getting better, I at least know my continents and reference points way better than before.

This Belize idea was foreign to me (pun intended). There was something about going to this place that spoke English but also spoke Spanish and Creole that truly intrigued me. This gave me the mentality that I could learn some Spanish and yet this country still provided the safety net of knowing English. This mentality was challenged upon arrival when we visited certain areas where only Spanish was spoken. By the time I was inundated with Spanish, my cultural horizons had been expanded. All I wanted was to learn and be around it more and more.

Other students my age and in my school had not really traveled much. Or at least I had not heard about it. Yet, there was a drive, from all the times and trips that I had completed with my parents, to make this specific trip possible. What I didn't know at the time was that it would push me to a place that would leave me marked for life. It would change the course of everything. I just knew I wanted to go.

Let me give you a little background of my youth. I was the only one, or depending on the year one of a select few, who was actively involved on Sunday and Wednesday nights and did not go to the city high school. This didn't bother me unless we played them in football. There was something about this dichotomy of youth that up until this point in high school caused me to hide certain characteristics of my personality. Though I was not shy, there were times when a majority of my conversations were only surface level. I was finally owning up to some parts of who I was. The idea of the mission trip was pushed even further because of this newly acquired sense of self, although my full personality would not become apparent until my junior year in college. One night after our youth meeting at church, I came home with this idea to go abroad. I let it sit for a few days thinking and pondering what I could do if I went, and would this be what I wanted to do.

At this point in my walk with God, I knew him, and understood his presence and the reason why we would go to church. I believed in Him and followed his commandments to the best of my ability. I grew up in the church. This was just my way of life. Separating my faith from my church's beliefs, as well as from my family beliefs, became a process of discernment and prayer. This process would slowly reveal itself and become apparent in my life. I was blind to the fact that he needed to be not only the ruler of my life, but the scale to which everything I said and did was measured. My actions had to match up to my words.

God needed to be my initial thought, conversation and relationship, rather than one I had on speed dial in case I needed him. That being said because I didn't really consult God for whether or not I should go except for maybe a quick prayer that I don't remember. I relied more on my gut feeling. At present, I find God working in my gut a bunch. Not that the other isn't needed or necessary, but Belize felt right.

Finally, remember I am an over thinker, I mentioned the trip to my parents and after some thought my dad said he would go with me. I remember the signup sheet being at the front of the youth gathering, in the dimly lit room downstairs. On the stage sat two stark white pieces of paper and in typical grid format, were names and phone numbers. These pages were extremely significant to me. Something deep within me knew I would never be the same. I remember vividly walking up and writing mine and my dad's names on those sheets that night. It felt so freeing. Something deep within me felt at peace and right about this decision.

Now the prep work for the trip had to begin, with fundraisers, programs, packing lists, and shots. We were off on the rampage, that is, getting ready for an international missions trip. I had my passport already. At that point I had been to Canada with my family, so that was one feat that I didn't have to cross; but the shots …. oh, the shots. If I remember correctly and maybe I don't for good reason, there were three shots that we were supposed to take for this trip. One was for a different type of hepatitis, one was for a tetanus because of course, mine at that point was out of date, and one was for something else. I remember the rounds for the hepatitis was in three different stages just like the ones that many of us had to get in middle school. They were bad but not terrible. Oh my goodness, one was for whatever it was, pain hides the memory of that shot's name. That shot hurt...really hurt.

I remember coming out of the doctor's office and thinking, "Man if mission trips are going to require this much pain, I am not sure if I want to go on them." Anyway, we survived, Barbie bandages and all, we came out of the doctor's office. I say "we" because luckily for me but not for him. Dad was not exempt from the shots, either. I prepared my bag full of supplies for Vacation Bible School (VBS) because I had been placed in charge of crafts. The clothes that I hopefully had enough guts to leave down there (because at this point my travel bags still consisted of everything but the kitchen sink). I also had to save room for the group t-shirts that we always were taking with us, in beautiful bright neon green, neon orange and gray colors.

Though I had been on many trips and was getting better at traveling, this one was an entirely different animal. This "animal" was compounded by the mental, spiritual and emotional thoughts. I attempted to prepare for the worst, hope for the best, and find God somewhere in between. There were forty-five of us going together. The preparation at the airport - getting us through security and customs and all that jazz, was a blur.

Praise God for Scott H. and his amazing leadership and encouragement that would lead me and others on this trip. At that time, he was my youth minister and the coordinator of this trip. This journey would cause us to have life-changing occurrences that would forever change our outlook and perspective on life as we knew it. During this moment, his wisdom in logistics was vital in getting all of us together. His wisdom still remains. A decade later, he still travels to Belize on a regular basis continuing missions, as now a senior pastor at a church. Scott would set a life course in motion for me. Later in life, I would assume Scott's initial role in my life and become the logistics coordinator for trips to Belize. God sure loves to bring a story full circle. Scott beautifully shared some of his story about missions and ministry.

> Since going on my first mission trip in 1994, I have traveled to many locations throughout the United States and abroad engaging in short-term mission work. Most of these trips have been sponsored by the local church under my leadership as a youth pastor or senior pastor. What has drawn me back to short-term mission experiences again and again has been the work of the Holy Spirit changing the lives of the beneficiaries of the mission work as well as the participants. We go on mission expecting that we will change lives, but it is God who changes us along the way. We come home thinking, seeing, and acting differently because God has grown our gospel imaginations larger.
>
> Wonderful things happen when we put ourselves outside the comfort of home territories and cultures, relying more fully on God's leadership and

provision. During one mission trip to Belize with First Baptist Church of Marion, NC, the phrase was coined "God in the details." Multiple times that week our team members were under-resourced for the needs that confronted us. Yet time and time again, the needed tool, the last loaf of bread, the generosity of a stranger was the answer to prayer. God took care of the details; everything we needed was remarkably provided. When we returned home, we found that we anticipated in a new and fresh way that God would provide in the same fashion, even in a land where big box stores overflow with every imaginable item and modern knowhow answers our dilemmas even before they occur.

The first time I traveled to Belize on a mission trip and returned home, I said to my wife, "Our house seems so much bigger!" After spending time with people who live in dramatically more modest, even meager, conditions, I was overwhelmed at how materially blessed I am. In fact, I was profoundly reminded that I waste more than most people in the world live on in a day's time. I found myself more attentive to the value of electricity and water, and to the need to put items in the recycling bin. I found myself less worried about buying the latest fashions when I have closets full of clothes. I found myself hugging my children and thanking God more. I found myself more thankful when I sat down to a meal at my dinner table. Somehow, I saw differently than I had before. The same old world I lived in was different because God had opened my eyes to appreciate what is provided to me more deeply.

Thinking differently about God's provision and seeing the world with greater stewardship resulted in many new efforts in the life of First Baptist Church of Marion. Two examples are most prominent. First, after traveling to Belize for several years in a row, a new opportunity came to First Baptist Church. A young Hispanic Baptist congregation was looking for a place to worship. They had hopes of building a church house of their own, but needed a temporary home. First Baptist Church welcomed the Spanish-speaking, immigrant congregation into our lives and agreed to partner with them, including allowing the full use of our church campus and vehicles. The Hispanic children attended First Baptist Church's Sunday School classes so that they could learn better English while growing in Christian faith. I believe that the ongoing mission trips to Belize helped First Baptist Church to see God in this opportunity and to rest in His guidance, sharing what we have with our immigrant neighbors.

A second example is the formation of a free medical clinic in our community, an effort heavily led by medical professionals who serve annually in Belize with our mission team. These doctors and nurses became passionate about caring for those with little access to medical care in Belize, a developing country with vast numbers of isolated villages. When the medical team came back to Marion, their thinking and vision were changed. They recognized that some of their own neighbors lived without proper medical care. This was a reality that these medical providers had always known. However, with new gospel-fueled imaginations, they saw a way to make a difference, to provide a faith-based clinic where financial need would never be a barrier to care. I believe the ongoing medical mission trips to Belize helped propel the formation of the free medical clinic. This local organization became a way for these medical professionals to be on mission every week right in their own community.

With these experiences and many more, I am reminded of a favorite verse from the Prophet Isaiah: *I am about to do a new thing; now it springs forth, do you not perceive it? I will make a way in the wilderness and rivers in the desert* (43:19). God is always doing new things in our midst. The question is, "Do we see it?" Short-term mission experiences help us to break away from our normal lives and patterns allowing us to see and think and do in fresh ways. These spiritual breakthroughs are themselves new things born of God. These mission trip revelations are not our own doing; they are God's doing. Such Spirit-filled imagination is God at work in our lives, making us and the world around us new through Christ who makes all things new."

Those words from Scott really sum up what missions means to me now.

When we finally took that flight, everywhere we turned there was another person in our t-shirt and you could move around quite easily to different seats on the plane. The flight seemed as if it took forever. I believe this was partly because of our excitement about the trip and partly because I had not flown many times or that far before. Once we landed in Belize City, we exited the plane via stairs that led down to the runway. Then we were directed to the terminal. We made our way in to find and rummage for all our personal bags and supplies. Then we began waiting in the customs line. I remember in the airport there was a guy playing music that I had not heard before. This was the initial cultural change that I experienced. Once we had our items collected, we began the process of trying to get outside.

After customs on our way out of the terminal and baggage claim, porters tried many times to take our bags. A few of them actually grabbed our bags to carry them a mere twenty feet to the outside of the airport where we would wait for our rental vehicles. After bickering and bargaining with a little money, all of our travel bags and participants were on the side of the road out in front of the airport. We waited as two Isuzu Trackers and two fifteen-passenger buses were rented and brought to us to act as our transportation for the week.

I remember we even took meat which were we going to cook for our group, in large coolers filled with ice - something that we could never do today, but at the time it was cheaper. We didn't have to worry about getting this supply at the camp where we were staying, and that was a huge relief. I am very thankful that this airport experience was not the same experience that happened on later trips to Belize. The porters are now somewhat regulated and can no longer enter the customs area at the airport. They have improved measures of security in other ways. People like Joan work upstairs at the airport restaurant. She makes your traveling experience wonderful. Whether you are waiting on your food that is delicious or another flight, she presents you with a hug and a smile. Other airport officials are amazing and make the process wonderful.

I do not remember the loading process, or how we managed to get all of our stuff in those vehicles. I do remember the drive, as we were behind one of the vans in an Isuzu Tracker. We would be going fifty-five on the road. All of the sudden of the heads of the people in the van in front of us would hit the ceiling, and we would slam on brakes because they "had warned us" that a speed bump was up ahead. There was no sign to tell us, or if there was, it was a hundred feet in front, behind the bump, or right at it, never in the same place. Finally, after a trek south, we made it to our camp.

I was surprised by the accommodations that we had within this country. Remember this was my first out of country experience (sorry, Canada, you don't count in this regard). Walking into a camp that had bunk beds and fans and running water (at points), I was excited. However, it did not distract me enough from seeing the world that revolved right outside the camp. Each day coming in and out, we passed a house where there was a child who was always outside or peeking outside. This child was either naked or with an only shirt on. I remember a few people being able to get this picture of the child peering out around the door frame. Yet, I didn't get one or need one because this image was ingrained in my mind from the moment that I saw it. This hit my core. How does a child not have a shirt, a literal shirt, that they can wear every day?

The children in these homes only know the area around their home for the first many years of their life. The likelihood that they have been more than a mile from their house (unless they have had the money to ride a public bus) is not very likely. I just think of how many things are often at the fingertips of American children today. Don't get me wrong; there is poverty and great need in the United States, but just think of the resources that we have. Funding for underprivileged programs, museums, camps, aquariums and zoos are available. Science centers, 4H clubs, and others are offered to children. People in other countries don't even have these places to go even if they had the money. This poverty struck a chord in me. I am still trying to figure out my role in breaking this cycle.

The cycle still exists but I can pour on love and adoration for the people who are oppressed. Another form of oppression that we faced was in the lack of clean water.

One of the hardest things for me to understand was why we could not drink the water in this country. Why could I not flush the toilet paper? What was so different that made this not possible? To solve the water problem, or at least sustain us for the week, we had to drink out of large five-gallon water jugs that we made sure were filled each day. That week we went through over 32 five gallon buckets of water, just within the camp alone. The number still haunts me. Then we would also have to cook with this bottled water. Our showers were conducted with rain water ... literally.

There was a huge black container in the back of the camp where all the rain water ran off the roof and was funneled to the container, then funneled to the shower heads. It was great to see how they could be so resourceful. For the first few days, there was something wrong with this container. If I remember correctly it was day three before I got a shower. Something so simple as a shower that I always took for granted became the most difficult project during this time. Oh, how I preserved that water.

When washing my hair, the water was on for the shortest amount of time possible. Then I quickly turned the water off. I had just enough water to get my hair wet enough so I could work a very small amount of shampoo through it. Standing in the shower wet, and cold because there was no hot water, was the only time you were cold during the entire trip. Then turning on that water so softly and gently, not to waste a single drop, there was this mad dash to reach every part of your body in 2.5 seconds because you wanted to use the water wisely, but also hope and pray that after everyone took a shower that day, that there would be enough water for you to take one the next day - something we never had to worry about in the states. In moments like these, God brought me closer.

The next weird thing that I noticed was that we had to brush our teeth with our bottled water. Let me remind you, we were still not off the training grounds. This was crazy to me. I was not used to carrying around a bottle of water and making sure that I knew where it was at all times (much like many of our cell phones today), I was constantly checking on the bottle of water. Was it full? Did I need more? Was something in it? Did I put the lid on? The list goes on, on, and on, but there we all were at the sinks with our bottle, toothbrush and toothpaste in hand, reminding each person that we were not to drink the water. So far so good. Just like the wrong water in this instance could make us sick, drinking from the "wrong water" at home can have the same or worse damage. What are we feeding ourselves socially, mentally, and emotionally, and how is that making a difference in our personal lives and our relationships?

Waking up early each morning because, I was an early riser, I would be the first one out of our room and hear the rain that would be falling in the morning. We all slept with our feet and arms spread out on the beds jumping jack style, because that was the way that everything touched the least and you were the least hot. Though we had fans, the impact was just stirring hot air around, not cooling anything off. The rain would come in the morning and feel great, but the muggy atmosphere that would happen right afterward was always a challenge... going from rain to hot, humid, and heavy. If you have never felt heavy weather, this was it. It is hard to explain, but everything became more taxing, and you were not sure if you were wet with sweat, or mist, or what was going on.

Down to the kitchen I went. I got to spend several mornings there with the cooks of our group making breakfasts for the team, because remember, I was the first youth who was awake. The time making pancakes and other food was a time when I could be alone with God, hear the sounds of nature around me, and listen to him.

Then it was finally time to go out to the work sites. One site was very interesting. I thought I had seen poverty, and I had definitely read about it by this point in my life, but I am not sure if I had I ever truly experienced it. The people in the communities that we passed by, and in the towns and villages, were different. They were happy despite their lack of things. They were thankful despite their problems. They were spiritually hungry beside their physical deprivation. This caught me off guard and I still to this day do not know how much the sights and sounds of the first village impacted and still impact me and my faith today. Jesus was in the midst of the mundane. He was with them in their poverty. Children, adults, families, dogs, horses, and other animals walked around slowly and oblivious to their plight.

We drove up and parked in front of the only building in this community that had cinderblock walls, and I thought we were going to the house of a person who had a bunch of money. I thought we were going to use their house as a launch pad for whatever we did. Well, I was wrong. The cinder block house was not a house; it was the only church that this community had. The church had been closed down for a year, locked up and sealed. Setting foot on this ground was painful -spiritually painful because a house of God had been closed for a year since people did not have the resources to keep it up. It was also physically painful, as the amount of fire ants that seemed to be on this one piece of property depicted a horror movie. Each member of the group was tiptoeing around the site and trying to make it swiftly into the building that they were unlocking.

The boys were supposed to take out a few stumps of trees that were in the yard of this church, and they were caught in the midst of the fire of the ants and the fire of the sun. However, this did not stop them. I remember the next time I looked up they had one stump out and were on to another ready to work and do the jobs that they had come here to do. This happened as you would hear "Ouch" as they smacked their feet, and "Get them off of me" in the distance. I was working on setting up the crafts for Vacation Bible School, making sure I brought the right materials for that day and getting things ready for the children.

If you know my mother and family, this was very a fitting job for me to do. Separating out the crafts and getting everything that we needed ready was what was consuming my time. I remember the pews in the church were old wooden benches of various sizes and the front of the church held only a wooden pulpit stand. There may have been more, but my memories are not vivid. My concern was the 8x8 slab of concrete that was to the back left of the building. This is where the crafts would be conducted. This was my station. I do not remember what the slab of concrete was originally poured for, but I was thankful it was not the dirt, and thankful that we had a place to work.

We each worked as busy as the fire ants, getting ready for the days ahead. Now a group of forty-five people and vehicles attracted attention this church that had been closed for a year. Less than thirty minutes after our arrival there, people were walking by the church to see what was going on. They were wondering why so many people were standing outside of the doors and using tools that they had never seen before. This was a community that was brought water 2-3 times a week in the five-gallon buckets to use for everything- food, drinking, pets, showering, etc. A few came into the church to get out of the sun and I think mainly because of curiosity to see what the inside of this building looked like. God was working in this area. Our group worked very well together, and we were ready for the next day to start the VBS. That day came and went, and I do not remember many of the details, but that we slept well and still watched our water bottles. We had devotions that night, but nothing life-changing to me at that point, I was going through the motions of my first mission trip.

Day two in the village came, again I was up and ready to go. We loaded the vehicles and off we went. This time the drive to the village did not sting emotionally as bad, we grow accustomed to things very quickly. Our hearts have to be broken repetitively to remind us of our position and our calling to serve the least, lost and left out. We made it to the church and it was already unlocked with the doors open and ready for us to come in. This time there were children already waiting on us and playing in the ant-infested front yard. This time it was less daunting. This time it was different. Unloading all of us and everything that we brought with us, I proceeded to my 8x8 square to set up the craft for the day. The children would rotate around to different stations. I would be ready to share what we were doing and why we were doing it. It was going to be awesome... and it was. This day seemed to fly by and the next one came and went just like it.

Somewhere along the line, we were doing a craft that the children had to paint, and because of the confined area, one of the children knocked over a container of green paint on my tennis shoes. Something about this spoke to me. Their eyes got huge and they were afraid that I was going to be mad because they misused a resource that was not theirs. Though my amount of useable green paint became smaller, the care that they took when they were using their brushes to clean it off my shoe and paint it on to something and clean it off the cement, but make sure that stroke counted, was amazing. The use of the resources and the meticulous care of their creations astounded me. I could not be mad about the green.

I had those tennis shoes for almost a decade after the trip reminding me each how blessed and responsible I am for what I have and that to whom much is given, much is required. Typically, I would pull those shoes out to go mow, my yard because the shoes had become well worn. I always was thankful for a yard that I had to mow much less a lawnmower that I had to mow it with instead of a machete, and ant hills...but that is neither here nor there. It was little moments like these that began to change my mindset, my course, my direction of life and my lifestyle at large.

During the time that we were at the church, there was a point when one boy became the center of attention. I was still working in my craft area and oblivious to what was going on around me. All of the sudden his story and his heart caught my attention. The boy no older than nine was being paraded around like a king by some people in our group. I was thinking that it was because he did something well or was the first to accept Jesus...something along those lines. This time it was different. This time, this boy in a village and country we had never been to or heard of less than six months ago was wearing a shirt that was made by a father of two children that were on our trip for their Boy Scout Troop. We have no clue where he got the shirt or what happened to get this shirt (made personally by the local Boy Scout Troop from Statesville two years prior) to Belize.

This was crazy for me, and I did not realize at the time how much this story would mean to me or why it would matter. After much thought and prayer on the matter, I concluded that this was God's way of telling the entire group, or at least me, that we were supposed to be on this trip at this time, in that village meeting the needs of that child. This occurrence brought to me the understanding that my ways are not his ways. My thoughts are not his thoughts. I grew to understand the depth, height and breadth of God and his ordaining me to be there in that moment and place. I don't know the child's name or if he accepted Christ throughout the week that we were there. I do know that his impact of just being present while we were working was worth more to me in that moment that anything I could give, say, or do. It is moments like these that causes me to remember and see that missions is so important.

Another girl touched my life in a myriad of ways. My first impression of her was her quiet and sincere demeanor. She was not boisterous or loud in coming over to the church each day, but quietly watched and waited to see what each of us had going on. There were times where the glimmer in her eye was questioning what was happening around her, but you could tell that something had drawn her to this time and to this moment. As she took in her surroundings, I was stunned by her grace and her love. She lived right beside the church, and honestly, who knows if she had ever been outside of her community. I found myself drawn to her nature and love. Not being over the age of seven at the time she had very limited vocabulary due to both her lack of school and her shy personality. However, I was able to find out that her name was Evelyn.

Each day she would walk over wearing shorts, and her Pocahontas t-shirts, with her hair combed as best as it could be and many times up in a ponytail. Her hair was as dark black as the midnight sky and her eyes pierced your soul. She would come to craft day each day and just sit with her legs directly out in front of her (which I was instantly jealous of, because I could not do that). God did not give me the ability to touch my toes. Touching my toes is one thing I will ask God about when I get to heaven.) Evelyn would color her coloring sheet with meticulous care. She would lay the piece of paper on her knees and she bend over and stare at the sheet, choosing each color specifically for one part or another. If another child was using a color, she would not move on to something different; she would just wait until they were finished and use the next crayon. She knew what she wanted and she waited and made it happen.

I have many times over these years that have passed gone back and prayed, thought about her, and sent my love her way. I have wondered if she has a family, is still in the same village, is working somewhere, or has moved to a different area or county, as she is probably around twenty years old now. I probably will never find out. I have no idea what God has done with her life, and I pray that she is making a difference and impacting others. If her sole purpose was to impact my life for eternity, she did, and for that I am more than grateful.

This initial mission trip sparked a flame in my heart to serve God in as many capacities as I possibly can. Belize inspired me to think more about the resources that I consume and what I can use more wisely. This experience started a journey that will take a lifetime for me to finish. It brought me to a point of self-realization that when much is given, much is required. In the United States, much is required. What and how are we leveraging our resources to make a difference in our community around us or in the context of the greater world?

I was brought closer to God by going away. Closer to his call on my life, closer in relationship with him and his people and closer to listen to the still small voices that prompt me to make a difference wherever I am. God came near and heard me cry out in anguish for those who had less, and gave me a responsibility to be an advocate. I will always remember the initial joy that I saw within the community upon our arrival. This joy is within my heart, beckoning me to always remember God and truly cherish the little things, moments, and emotions.

New Orleans

People often think mission trips within the states do not make an impact internationally. Go to your neighbor down the street or someone just a mile away. I have done much research on Charlotte and surrounding areas, as well as various other cities and towns, and the number of international people living right at our doorsteps is astounding. Many people tell you about going to a place in the United States and come back saying it felt as if they were in a different country. If you are like me and have any type of accent - be it Northern, Californian, Texan, or Southern - you get recognized really easily when you speak in an area where your dialect is not the norm. This happens to me all the time. I am one of those people who take on accents easily and can often accentuate my Southern accent even when I don't realize it. New Orleans is no different. Louisiana is a state where the tea is sweet and the food is amazing. It is within this state that they have seen much hardship, yet they maintain their cultural identity really well.

In 2007, as a junior in college, I had the opportunity to go on a mission trip to New Orleans. This was a few years after Hurricane Katrina. Hurricane Katrina was the United States costliest natural disaster to date and one of the five deadliest hurricanes. Killing over 1,800 people, and costing over $108 billion in damage.[9] Katrina hit many areas in the Southeast, greatly affecting Louisiana, Mississippi and Alabama, and parts of Florida even though my visit was a few years removed from the hurricane, the effects of the damage were still widespread, both emotionally and physically. We arrived in New Orleans after needless to say a very long truck ride that began at 3:00 in the morning. It consisted of a round robin sleep and drive brigade and vehicle caravan. The three girls with me on that trip still have a very special place in my heart.

There was a large group of us going down from our school's chapter of Campus Crusade for Christ. I don't know if I was naive, or if they just did not tell me, but when we arrived it was very different than what I previously thought. I was not sure what to expect. We knew

---

[9] (The Top 5 Most Expensive Hurricanes, 1).

we were staying in some form of a hotel, but who knew what it would look like. Maybe I was thinking "Belize bunk bed" and hoped to have a fan. This was the style that was in my head. Well, much to our surprise, our school along with many other schools descended, on a very upscale hotel in the downtown district of the city. We were each given projects to work on throughout the week that we were staying, and had conference times to meet together as an entire unit in the evenings.

Staying at a hotel on the river was something I was not expecting. This trip from its inception was one that was a different nature. The hotel was only the beginning. We were able to walk around downtown and see the beauty of the city that had been quickly rebuilt. On our hours off, we were able to eat at really nice restaurants, experience jazz music, shop and enjoy our love for Cafe du Monde and their coffee and beignets. This created moments of joy and deepening of relationships. These times we were able to grow together with one another, experiencing salsa dancing in the halls of the hotel to vendors on the banks of the river. However, driving out to our work site created a depiction of the city that honestly I didn't desire to see.

We had two different projects. On one we went out to their warehouse. This building was broken down by any standards, and yet there were people who lived there. I remember our task was to make raised flower beds in the side yard and on the roof. We took leaves and piled them on the preexisting beds. Then somehow they had 12-18 inches deep of used coffee grounds that were brought there to be "recycled". This went on as the next layer, and then dirt on top of that. The cleaning and planting happened as the day drew to a close. The residents who we were working with us asked if we wanted to stay and have a bonfire and a music jam session, so of course we obliged.

I remember sitting in random makeshift chairs and a woman sitting on the steps of the building begin playing the guitar and singing. It was a night to remember. As we sat there, I was eating an apple that I had gotten from the hotel from breakfast and just packed away in my bag. If you know me, I am picky about my apples, and the crispier the apples are the better. Well, this apple was soft and not good (in my opinion). I took the first bite and I knew I was not going to finish it. The texture was something that I just couldn't handle. I asked one of the residents for the trash can because I did not want to litter, and they quickly took the apple from me pulled out a pocket knife and cut off the part that I took the bite from.

They proceeded to eat the apple until only the smallest apple core that I had ever seen was left. This brought me to my "humble knees" really swiftly. I was being picky about my apple, something that I had gotten for free from a "nice hotel", and yet the ones we were helping were in need. They lived in an area without having an inspection code for their building, or locks. They were focused on planting the ground to sustain their lives in the coming years and months. I was concerned about my mushy apple, not meeting my current hunger needs, and not littering.

Though the littering was a good concern, it should not have been my first priority. After this event occurred, the songs and the night brought a new perspective for this trip. The lyrics to the music sank in deeper. The stillness that was all around me brought a new reality of how chaotic the flood would have been in this area. It brought me to a new awareness of my humanity, my depravity and my ability to so easily get off track with my priorities and not focused on my relationship with God and the needs and priorities of others.

The second project was where we spent most of our time. This project that our group was given was to demolish a church in the lower Ninth Ward, the area of New Orleans which was the most impacted when the hurricane hit. For it was in this area that the walls had been breached by the water influx carried in by Hurricane Katrina. The utter devastation that we saw was gut wrenching the first time that we drove out to the site. Though two years removed, you could see places where houses should have been, but were now just plots of land. Then you would pass by a house a few blocks down the road that would still be semi standing, and each house would have a "x" on it with numbers written in various positions of the "x" as if the house had been searched when the waters were there. It was marked to show if people were found, dead, alive, or escaped. This was an amazing reality to me that this can and did happen and people's lives were literally torn apart by a natural devastation. My heart broke knowing that nothing could have been done to prevent this storm from happening. Yet, everyone with all of their being wished that they could have done something more.

We continued our drive just a few more blocks and turned left down the street. I remember passing by a few houses that had since been rebuilt. This came nothing close to the thriving community I knew this area once was. We stopped at this location and we all hopped out of our cars. The site before us was something indescribable. All we could see was debris. Someone met us at the site and told us that this area was a former church (which we would not have known). Our task that week was to clear off the plot of land so that the church could be rebuilt back in that same area. There was something was amazing about this task. Yes, it is weird to think that tearing down a church could be a part of God's plan. I could not help but ponder what he had planned for the new church, the people it would impact and the lives that the church could become home to in the future.

So there we were with a 20-30-foot-tall debris pile, a few shovels, some gloves, and some sunscreen. The wood that we could save, we stacked up and stored in a building on the same block. The broken and battered pieces all went to the curb, where we began to build an impressive pile of things for the city to eventually pick up. Among the rubble were Bibles, microphones, hymnals, and a few other odds and ends that we saved and set aside for mementoes. It was amazing to see the effort that went into this project, and to see how our team came together and made it happen.

Though this project was amazing, and I would not have traded my working at the church for anything, the entire week was trumped by one five-minute conversation that I had with a family on our free time walking around the downtown area of New Orleans. Later during the week of our stay, we were challenged to get cleaned up and go around praying for and talking to people in the city. At the time I thought this was weird. I will never understand the ways in which God would use a family I would meet. I could not tell you their names, unless I was lucky enough to write it on the back of a photo. However, if memory is correct, no photo was taken of this family.

Elizabeth Barnard

We were walking along the streets near the water in New Orleans when this couple walked by with a daughter in a stroller and another daughter. You could tell by the couple's walk, demeanor, and dress that they were down on their luck. We asked if we could talk with them for a few minutes, and they obliged. After introducing ourselves and telling them why we were there, the conversation began to open. The mother said they had lived in New Orleans all of their lives and they were in the city when the hurricane happened. The amount of terror that was in her eyes years after the event was something I hope I never experience. As she began her story, the details all ran together in my mind. I was focused on her body language and her face. I did not know or understand how she could still be smiling through it all. When I tuned back in, she was talking about her youngest daughter - the one in the stroller. I had noticed but didn't really pay attention that the daughter was in shorts and her legs and arms were discolored in different spots.

The mother said that they were in the water, and something within the water that led to an infection on her child's skin. She went on to say that these two children who were talking and giggling with us were not their only children. The other children had been displaced to different cities and a few in different states to live with relatives. I think there were five or six children within this family. She mentioned two, if not three, places where the children were staying. They could not all live in the hotel that they were living in (still two years after the hurricane). She also mentioned that the money that the government had given them would not cover the expenses needed to build another home similar to the one that they previously had.

This is not a bash on the government or how funds sometimes are misallocated, but a human realization that often things happen out of our control that change the course of our lives. It is how we respond to these circumstances that proves the type of people we are. I was shocked. How could she be away from her family? Why didn't she move? What happened? Why stay in New Orleans? What was the deal? It took me a long time to realize that she stayed not because of trying to rebuild a house, not because their living conditions were the same or that she wanted to be near family - all of which she wanted. She stayed because she hoped and dreamed for a brighter tomorrow, another house to call a home, a family that would be together again with a community that had been rebuilt and relationships that had been restored. She hoped for a future.

As I stared into the eyes of the child in the stroller with the burn marks on her arms and legs, I was almost in tears. Seeing the smile of a child eating a lollipop that we had given her, who had experienced more trauma in her life by the age of two than I had in my life up to that point, astounded me. I was thrown into this thought process of how God uses so many of us to impact one another in ways we never even realize and in times we never knew we needed.

We asked to pray with the family, as that was our original intent. We began praying for the safety of the ones they were away from, the quickness of the government and volunteers to restore some areas, and the protection of their family, health, and new home to come. As we finished praying, I thought we would be done and move along our way back to the hotel, as it was getting time for our group session. However, yet again, the family shocked me. They asked if they could pray for us and what we were doing in the area and our safety home.

It is through this experience that I truly felt God's presence and peace in a place that I had previously not known. It is in this time that I understood how God unites us near and far over things that we never thought possible. It is amazing to see how God, great and powerful that he is, watches over the intricate details, leading our team directly to the lady and her family that we hopefully blessed, but who definitely blessed others. I love a God that is intricate in the details.

In this moment that we "went away closer", we found more hope in our future, knowing our future with Christ was and is solidified through the death and resurrection of his son. We found hope in knowing that whatever the circumstances of life, be it natural disasters or something else, this does not change our acceptance into his kingdom if we accept him in our lives. We go away for moments in time to draw closer to God and his people.

New York

One of the most different mission trips that I took was chaperoning a group of high schoolers to go to New York City. Yep, I was being placed partially in charge of a group of teenagers. Scary, huh? The beginning of the trip was much like the rest. We had to prepare and pack and get all of our supplies together. We had to make sure that everyone would be able to make it to the train, because, yes we were taking a train from North Carolina to New York. This was a fun idea. The train did not leave until 2 am and it was running late. The train had hit a cow (literally) but that is beside the point. Still, poor cow. Once we got on the train, we were almost instantly asleep. For the first few hours, silence filled our train car. The roar of the wheels on the tracks gradually rocked us into a deep slumber. Soon enough the morning light would begin to wake us up. We then began a chatter that would not stop until long after we returned home.

Finally arriving at the station in New York, we filed out of the train onto a subway with all of our luggage. Many of the youth were getting their first experience on the subway and in a huge city. Our task that week was twofold. One part of the group would be working in the Teen Challenge Center that was in an upper part of the city. The other group would be working at a food pantry, organizing and sorting food on the shelves, as well as dividing and making sandwiches for the days while we were there. I was a part of the second group, so off to the food pantry we went.

The first day we were each given hair nets, aprons and gloves and we had to separate and bag bagels. This would not be hard on a regular day, but everything that happened at this pantry seemed to happen on scales that were beyond my imagination. When we walked into a room where we were to separate the bagels, there was a huge metal food preparation table in front of us and much to our surprise, in the corner of the room was not one but six to eight large Rubbermaid containers full of bagels from a bagel shop nearby. Now these were the previous day's bagels that they could not sell. If they did not give them to the pantry, they would have to throw them away.

New attention was brought to how people at restaurants get rid of their food which they can no longer legally sell, but at the same time is not bad, old or stale. It started each of us thinking of the different ways and times when we have had something that was good to eat but did not finish it and just threw it away, and how wasteful we have been in the past. I remember being told in middle school on a consistent basis that I was wasteful with what I did not eat of my lunch. Most of the time it was usually finished, yet the times it wasn't, I was told that kids in Romania would love to have my food because they were dying of starvation. This may have been true, and why they picked Romania, I have no idea. After taunts of this day by day, I finally said why don't you ship it to Romania and see if it is edible for those kids once it gets there. I fully support the end of the world's malnutrition. My little lunch in North Carolina was not going to stop malnutrition in Romania. At that point I did not have any knowledge of Romania or if they were struggling with malnutrition. Memories of this over and over again with restaurants and the amount of food we as American's eat ran through my head as we were in the pantry. That is a longer rant for another day.

As we separated everything, from blueberry, to cinnamon raisin, and bagged the bagels into groups of five for the next night's guests, I pondered where we fit into this larger scene. Knowing we were leaving in a few days and new groups would come in to fill our role of separating and organizing, how could we leave an impact both there and when we got home? We did not ever really answer this question, and I think it is something that truly plagues us as a society now. We don't know, how, what, or where to help, so we take the back seat and resolve to do nothing. The church body has turned a blind eye for too long. Not cool, society, not cool! Well, our bagels were separated, our time was over and so off we went to head back to our hostel.

Our time at the pantry wasn't over. The next day arrived, and I was assigned to a new team. Never before in my life have I seen a gallon size jar of peanut butter and gallon size tub of jelly. Never have I ever made that many peanut butter and jelly sandwiches. But that was our task, "Make sandwiches, until you are through," and that is what we did. Over and over again that is what we did. I had peanut butter up to my elbows because of how big the jar was and how you had to get everything on the sandwich just the correct way and somehow hope that we could get it in the bag without it being too messy.

We went through thirteen loaves of bread one day, making and bagging sandwich after sandwich. While one team was on this, another team of our group was separating and dividing all the food items. They were stocking the pantry box after box, and the team went through each shelf organizing as they went along. When they finished stocking the shelves, we had finished making the sandwiches. Thinking we had done a very good job, I was amazed to see how hard the youth had worked to get it all accomplished. We left for the day excited, knowing that our hard work would pay off for the next day and we would not have to make sandwiches and could do something different, something (in our minds) better than slabbing two pieces of bread with jelly and peanut butter.

Evening went and morning came and then it was the third day (sound familiar). We went back in the pantry the next morning and wanted to see how many of our sandwiches people had picked up from the pantry that previous night. Much to our shock and our slight dismay all thirteen loaves worth of our sandwiches had been distributed to people who came by during the night. It was amazing to see the need that was so evident in this area and in the United States in general. The youth and I spoke about our own homeless shelter, and it made us more aware of the needs that we did not choose to see when we were home. This was how we went away closer.

This sandwich-making and need was brought more to reality for me as our church did a summer program collecting and distributing sandwiches to those in need. In our small area of North Carolina, it was amazing to see how big of a need people had for food over the summer. This making of sandwiches in New York was brought closer when we would make them standing in lines with gloves on, under a tent, passing it out to people. We would create a relationship with those who received the sandwiches, praying with them and leading some to Christ. This program locally showed me once again how important it is too often to do the mundane tasks that are before me, to make the biggest difference. I had underestimated the importance of this task in New York, and again I underestimated the effect sandwiches would have locally.

As I grew to understand more about New York City and the populations which call this location home, I was not surprised to see the large number of populations and people groups present in this area. According to the latest census in April 2010, New York City has a population of just over 8 million people. In those 8 million people, people are categorized into eight main races. They are American Indian/Alaskan native, Asian, Black or African American, Hispanic/ Latino, Hawaiian or other Pacific Islander, some other race, two or more races, and White. White is the largest race, taking up 44.6%, next was the Hispanic/Latino with 27.5%, third is black/African American 25.1%, some other race at 16%, followed by Asian 11.8 %, with two or more at 2.1%, with the American Indian at .4 % and lastly the Hawaiian/Pacific Islander at .1%.[10] The most staggering statistic in the whole region is that 16% consider themselves to be from some other race.

The question that continues to arise is, what does "some other race" mean? While the answer may not be provided, they are still considered a race and represent a rather large part of New York. Along with the variation of races, they also represent a vast number of people groups. There are over 75 nations represented in the New York area, according to the North American Mission Board.[11] Each of these nations represents at least one people group, but they also represent at least one, but most of the time many, cultures. There are also over 130 different languages spoken at home by these same people.[12] The diversity seen in New York is unmatched anywhere else in the United States. So when dealing with the City of New York and its problems, it is essential to consider the population and the diversity that exists. Why do these statistics matter? They matter because they remind us that cultures and religious customs different from ours, are continuously around us, present in our daily

---

[10] (*Wikipedia*, New York Demographics).
[11] (*People Groups*).
[12] (Ibid.).

encounters and endeavors, having an impact on us, even if we don't realize it.

This diversity is not confined to New York. Everywhere we look, we are surrounded by people who have walked a different path, often in a different place than we have. Some of my best friends are from other cultures or countries, and it just makes my life richer. It is from this diversity on this trip to New York, this research and the continuing situations in which I find myself, that I found we are constantly surrounded by opportunities to meet, reach and walk with others. We have the ability to share our journey and help them see and meet the God that created us all. We are given a responsibility to be the light to whoever is around us, locally regionally and internationally.

Israel

Israel was an entirely different breed of a trip. For those of you who don't know, part of my story consisted of divinity school, where some of this comes in. I was finishing up divinity school with a concentration in Intercultural Studies, I like international relations, international politics (I can't believe I just said that), and of course, international places and people. Each year the divinity school offers a trip to go to Israel and either Turkey or Egypt or Greece and Ephesus. This is to see the life and journey of Christ or the life and journey of Paul.

Of course, since the inception of my divinity school experience, I knew that prior to my graduating, I would take one of these trips. It was required in my mind to make this happen. So this signup, unlike the initial Belize sign up, was a no brainer. My name was quickly one of the first people on the list and if I remember correctly I was the first one to put a deposit down for this trip, because I knew I was going. The world almost said differently. With political unrest, there were times leading up to the trip that we were not sure if we would be able to go. Praise the Lord that when the time came to leave, we were allowed to go, and things had settled down in the regions where we were headed.

Off started the longest voyage that I take on a plane. Remember, I am still getting better, but the long flights are boring and cramped. Yet each time, the flights are well worth the joy that we receive in the places that we go. As we landed in Istanbul, we had a final flight to Tel Aviv. When we made it there, we were picked up by our guide and soon to be a great friend... let's call him Dean. He was on the bus telling us things which we were going to see, giving us information. Already a sponge even in my half asleep layover and jet lagged stage, I soaked up every piece of information he stated. We had the wonderful joy to be traveling with some of our professors also, which added layer upon layer of knowledge and wonderful purpose and meaning to the trip. Without them, the trip truly would not have been the same.

The stories from this trip could fill multiple books on the moments, thoughts, and conversations that I had with Dean and others to make this the trip of a lifetime. Yet a few stories highlight the ways in which God spoke to me and how he continues to speak to me in my everyday life. Over the course of the next few days, as Dean would take us around to different locations, there were moments where we would walk into an area and it would be prefaced with "This is where it is believed to be…". Can you believe that during biblical times there was not a GPS code that was imprinted into scripture during points where Jesus did his ministry? How rude. I am totally kidding.

Some of the beauty of the scripture, and especially while I was over there walking around, is that some of the events and occurrences in the bible have a general location, but not a specific place. The beauty of this for me is that we in our human nature would try to make shrines and idols of these different places, but without knowing exactly where these are we are, leave these as disputable matters. Some questions need a definitive answer; some need a conversation. Not being able to be in the exact location of an event does not change or waive my faith. In all honesty it makes my faith stronger. I am able to see the areas in which events happen and allow the Holy Spirit and my imagination to direct me to create a visualization of the event that is better than any place I would pay to go and see because "someone special at some point walked there". Taking in the sights, sounds, smells and people watching while we were all across the city was what made the trip for me. We were given moments to just read scripture, ponder, reflect and listen to what we were being told, what we were feeling. There were times when tears were shed; other times when we were able to laugh at our experiences and our misunderstandings and become closer with God and with our group.

While we were on our trip to Israel, there were times in which God was seen all over the place whether we were at the sea or in the desert. Just being there, walking where He walked and sensing the spirit in the literal places that He had been, created a freedom that is unexplainable.

There was a time during the trip that we were each having the opportunity to be baptized in the River Jordan. Like so many other others, the tourist hype of going into this part of the river was similar I would suspect to what most who have been baptized in this area experienced in the moment. First, we were driven to the separate changing rooms for the guys and girls. This was after we had picked up our robes what we were to wear for baptism. We had to buy our baptism robes, and Dean knew someone in town that we could buy them from for a reduced price. The robes were all white except for an interesting depiction of Jesus's baptism right in the front in a 12x12 square.

After changing into our bathing suits and robes, we walked down to the river by the cascading steps. There was a sense of peace about this time and this place. There were small wading pools and areas that were literally fenced off to walk into the water for your baptism. Fencing in the water did not create for our ideal baptism scene, as you literally peered through the gates and holes of the fences, but it didn't really matter. There were otters and fish swimming around, which some of the group found terrifying and somehow it brought me closer to home than I realized. I grew up with water in front of my house and the occasional beaver or muskrat. Two thousand miles away, I was right outside my front door. This not only helped my nerves, but connected me even deeper to a God who is with me wherever I go all the time.

Our baptisms they were grand, as you could imagine; however, this was not the moment that I want to write about. There were no doves descending, no pausing of the earth's atmosphere, and no audible voice from God saying he was well pleased. At least not for me. There was this sense of purpose and "right place, right time" mentality which for Tyler, we will see became literally apparent. It was a few moments right the baptisms. The songs had been sung and we just stood around watching the river flow down the banks and others walking back and forth down the river. Some were drying off, others just talking with one another and watching the river, and others were gathering their clothes to walk back up to the dressing rooms and change. There was this tiny pool of shallow water that was up at the top near our area. This area which was four to six inches deep had small fish swimming around. This was something that I would not have noticed, expect there was Tyler.

Tyler had been watching the fish swim around and all of the sudden there was a brief moment that we saw Tyler diving for a fish. He actually caught one! This was so hilarious to watch. Joy on his face and the fish in his hand. He had caught something in a place that meant something more here than anything else. Tyler's catch resonated with me deeply. Something about the entire baptism that we had just experienced completely shifted my perspective.

This fish resonated with me. I was the fish. I was the one who wanted the shallow relationship with God. I was the one who was small and was afraid to go deep. I was the one who wanted to bask in the sunlight and get out of the walls that were confining me, but did not confine me enough to push back and make a change. This was huge. You can see the representation that I am about to make of Tyler and his similarities of God being able to get messy and willing to dive into the situation. Though this is cheesy, this, allowed me to see that God wanted me to break the barriers that I had allowed others to create and that I had created myself. I had to be willing to be a small fish, in a big river allowing the current to take me on a journey that I could not foresee and find questions and answers that I would never expect or imagine. This would require me at points to swim hard, to think I was overwhelmed and incapable to continue.

At this point I would begin to see more of the adventure that God had planned for me, the ways in which he was calling me to move though seemingly stupid, mundane, mediocre, or random events. Everything seemed to work together for his plan and his purpose. I was the one who had to be consistently caught by God in silly and often funny looking ways because I was the one who was not looking towards his plan and prerogative, but my own. Looking back, that water spoke to me in a multitude of ways. Though hindsight is always better, the peace that this hindsight brings, propels us into a future that is bright and wonderful tomorrow, not void of challenges but definitely not void of God. It is in that way that I go away closer to him.

Another moment that will always be near and dear to me about Israel was the time when we were in Jerusalem and we were going to stop by a store that sold trinkets and items made from olive wood that this area is known for. Those who were on our trip, and are reading this, immediately know where I am going on this story. Sit back and remember. As we were about to stop, the store owner - who had become friends with our trip leader - hopped on the bus to give a brief overview of what was going on in the store, the way that things worked and the way that they created the items that they sold. The joy that emanated from his face as he welcomed us into his store and introduced us to his family was something I will not soon forget. He then treated us as he prayed for each of us on the bus and then sang part of a beautiful hymn.

When we got off the bus we went inside to see more things made from olive wood in one location than I have ever seen before or since. The business that was family run was more inviting than most places I have seen. As we were standing around looking at the items that ranged from fifty cents to thousands of dollars, we grouped around the center of the room to look at some of the items that the family members were showing us. I just happened to be dressed in a white flowing shirt that day. Within a few minutes I had a halfhearted-half real request for marriage and an offering of 500 goats and 100 camels to my family. My family would have flipped. Luckily and honestly, I could say that my family had a goat already and that was enough. School, not marriage, had to be a priority. Total kidding aside the people in this store, after knowing us for only a few minutes treated us like family - joking, laughing, and just caring much as you would hope any family would. This is a memory that I will always cherish. Though I found this funny, it was crazy to see that this kind of tradition of bartering for marriage was still in use today in that region. It is amazing to see how the cultures of one area can reflect the times for thousands of years ago, and then a few minutes later, they pull out the technology that represents the 21st century by using their smart phones and computers.

We each bought our items and took our pictures buying a bracelet and a set of praying hands. That sits in my bathroom on my vanity and reminds me of this simple moment. Others bought different items - nativity sets, jewelry, and ornaments. I wanted to buy more, but somehow the praying hands signified everything. It showed me that this trip represented God's unconditional love for me. This reminded me, He has a consistent cry for love and relationship with each of us. We loaded back on the bus and proceeded to our hotel for another night in Bethlehem. However, the next morning news would come that would rock our world. When we woke up and went downstairs to have our breakfast we were faced with the news that the store owner, whom we had just met the day before and blessed us in so many ways, had suddenly passed away from a heart attack.

This was a shock to all of our systems. Our leaders had sensed prior to leaving to pack a black shirt in their bags (which they would not have normally done). This shirt would be used to go and visit the family during this time of grief. The traditions of this country were different when it came to funerals than ours, as you would expect. I found out through this process that the grieving lasts for a year, and that you were not supposed to touch or move the things of the beloved. For us in the States, this is different in that many times we want the things of our loved ones out of sight out of mind quickly. They keep them in plain view. Then another interesting thing was the men and the women of the family were separated at the funeral home, not to be with one another. It is amazing to learn and hear of the traditions that are happening all around us. This is why I love traveling and cultures so much you see things that you did not know happened unless you looked.

After all of this, we spent some time going to the Garden of Gethsemane. The aura of this place was something that I can't really explain. There was a weight to this area that made you whisper, behave, and pay attention all the more to the things that were going on around you. Not knowing if it was the specific grave or not, at least we knew it was in the general area. We each took a solemn turn peeking our head in and turning around in a grave that would have been similar to the one where Jesus would have been laid to rest. The density of the rock, the weight of what this meant, all settled in really fast. After this brief time, we took a few more moments to pause and reflect on what would have happened. Stopping to think about the Easter story, we paused and reflected about this story's weight on humanity. The fact that this death was something that was so common to this time, this burial was one that was just like any other, but the difference, the thing that changed everything, was that it did not stay this way.

So many song references could be inserted here, *Up from the Grave He Arose*, and the list goes on and on. But it was during this time that we all circled around one another when it hit us; it hit me. He died for me, just me, my sins, my shame, and all of that is taken care of and I am free. The cool thing is that He died for each of, us both individually and collectively.

The communion meal was set on this warm and sunny day around the tomb and we sat there. Sooner than I ever imagined, the tears began to flow down my cheeks, as well as many other cheeks as the reality and weight of this set in. I remember having my friend George sitting right beside me and as we sang songs after the communion meal was shared, I was given tissues (because if you know me I am not a pretty crier). Then we all just joined one another, some with arms around each other, some holding hands singing to the one who created, and redeemed all in that place at that moment. What a powerful message that he gives us each Easter, but also daily, that we are clean by his blood and yet he still wants us to know love and worship him. This is something of which I am truly in awe.

This may seem as if it is just another off-the-wall story that I am telling you about some random experience that I had in some foreign place. But this, like the other stories, was something more than that. This was an insight into time and how when we least expect it, something out of the ordinary (both good and bad) can happen. It is a time when we can see that God is with us in the midst of it all. There is a time during all of this that we can see how we are here for a moment and gone tomorrow, whispers in the wind daring to hold on for the brief moment to make an impact and to leave a legacy. This is what I gained from my family that no matter how short our encounter is with someone and no matter the differences between you, there is a time where we can be each impacted eternally by others. I pray that you are the joyful moment for someone that you just met or for someone that you have known your whole life. Be willing and open to tell others what they mean to you and do not go to bed angry because we are not even promised today. What a great reminder of the love that was shown to this family around the globe and the impact that our leaders had on me by taking time out of their day to go and see the family that to them had become such dear friends. When we have gone away, how will we have impacted others to bring them closer to Christ?

Europe

"We need to do the Jesus' way for us and for our lives and our calling."

-Christine Caine

This trip was different from all the rest of the trips that I have spoken about. This trip was not mission oriented. It was for pleasure, yet in the midst of the trip, I found that God had a mission for me while I was interacting with those who were all across the world. The trip consisted of visiting eight different countries in Europe by bus. We went to all the major sites and had taken pictures in places that most people only dreamed of. Our tour guide was from Europe, but our bus driver was from Australia. The way that he maneuvered through the old streets impressed me more than I ever expected. I hopped on the bus with my best friend and eight from NC State University Alumni. Then we were combined with forty others from all over the world. One of the girls from State that neither my friend nor I knew, we met in the restroom of the Raleigh airport. She just happened to be traveling by herself to Europe two days earlier, like we were, and so immediately we bonded.

So off we loaded two days later on a bus that would be our home for the next almost two weeks. I never in my life thought I would be the "bus tour" type of trip person. As we were under way we began the process of introducing ourselves over the intercom on the bus, telling where we were from and what we did. God began to use those moments to open conversations. As I stood up, I shared I was from the great State of North Carolina in the United States and I was in graduate school for religion. This was easier than to say at the time I was getting a Divinity degree in Intercultural Studies. Others would ask me what that meant and it was a difficult process explaining it to the detail it deserved. So there it was out there - I was the "religion" girl.

You have to understand Europe and this stage within the historical religious context. Though religion played a huge part of its creation and culmination of many kingdoms, wars, and legacies, going through a period of religious depravity. This post Christian mindset is still true and where I fear and see America heading. The churches that are there are being transformed into museums, architectural wonders and new venues for things from restaurants to you name it. The church in Europe is in desperate need of a revival.

Due to the religious history of Europe, we went into many of these places that held deep roots in changing the people's way of life. Notre Dame, other chapels and the work of famous painters and artists in places such as the Sistine Chapel framed out trip to these places. Our guide would go over a brief history of how the places came to be, and then we were left to see and imagine and wonder on our own. The awe and wonder God allowed me to have while I was walking in the Roman Colosseum, parading down the halls of the Vatican, or listening to the priest conduct a small but very sacred service at Notre Dame at times almost brought tears to my eyes. With each location I seemed to find myself paired off with a different member of our bus group. Walking around the halls and sharing our thoughts and emotions created great openings in conversations with the banker from Dubai, the couple from South Africa, the doctors from California, the accountant from Canada, and the list goes on and on.

Because of the friendships that I made on this trip, I have had the opportunity to pray with and for many people I met. I have kept in touch and seen the work that the South African couple does with their church. I have emailed and talked on the phone about life's scary next steps for the Canadian accountant, and then I have welcomed many babies via *Facebook* many babies. It is from these experiences that I have seen the ways in which other cultures integrate with one another and thrive off of international experiences. Each one of us on the trip was from a place other than Europe. This was not our socioeconomic context, and whether we had visited these locations before or not did not change the fact that we were impacted by other's views, emotions and realities.

Belize 2.0

Who knew that God, almost a decade later, would call me back to the country where I went on my first international mission trip. At first when I felt this nudge, I was very shocked. I thought many times about the people and the place and I knew deep down I would be called back to this land and this people, but how, when, why, never was really clear for me. Somehow God showed me a way in which he wanted me to go. I had never been so nervous, excited, skeptical, or ready. I am not sure how you can mix all of those emotions together at one time but it was a concoction that brought me to my knees many times, making me question whether I was I going to follow God and his leading, or turn my back on him. The scary part was that the decision was mine to make. Missions in general has a tendency to do that to you. It takes you to a place out of your comfort zone. It questions your skills, quality of work, and every aptitude that you thought you had. Yet, if you remain in this awkward and inadequate feeling over and over you will see Christ's workmanship. This workmanship is seen not only working around you but working in and through you. You must experience this!

This calling, required me to quit my job, (yes, I am one of those called to quit because of missions). I remember like it was yesterday, walking to the pastor's study, oddly not nearly as nervous as I thought I was going to be. The conversation began about my plan and my impending resignation. Our discussion about the next steps was more equipping and empowering than I ever imagined. The pastor sensed my calling and knew God had plans for me, plans different from those I originally thought. His God-given insight was a true witness yet again to God using people to impact the journey I was called on.

I was leaving a great job with some awesome co-workers and amazing children, yet I knew God had another plan. Though no major tears were shed in the pastor's office, they streamed down my face as I told my children's committee about my decision. God was calling me from something very good to something great, and my responsibility was to follow his call.

Something about all of this did not feel as if I were leaving anything or anyone. This community was supporting me, praying for me, and encouraging me, though tears were shed in the process. It was this building upon the foundation which was already laid by so many others and previous journeys God had sent me on. I was able to see how God was in this and was using the skills from everything else I had accomplished to make me equipped for the journey that was ahead. I could not wait.

So after my resignation was turned in and all ducks were lined up as well as they could be, I set out for another Belizean adventure that would be nine weeks longer than any foreign travel I had done before and more exciting and revealing God to me, as well as God revealing me to myself. You can guess what was first packed, my blanket from the very beginning of the story. I was going away closer. Needless to say it would come in handy on the nights that were cold after the sunburned days, or the occasional nights that we would have air conditioning in our rooms and we would run it full blast-not because we needed it, but because we could.

Off I ventured by myself after leaving my tearful parents at the airport counter (while shedding a few tears myself), onto a plane with straightened hair, that would not be seen for the next two months because of the humidity. Thank goodness for two things: one, I had a short flight, and that the flight was direct. This required me only to worry about getting to one place, and then God would take care of the rest. I had the row to myself on the plane, which allowed God to come in and sit on either side of me and talk during the entire flight. Trust me, during this time we talked. Maybe just in my head there were times he and I sat in silence surrounded by his comfort. I went over all the things that I could experience, all the things that I hoped would happen, and all the excitement that had happened leading up to this day. I was exhausted from it all and found comfort and knowledge that he would restore everything. I even was able to sneak in a quick flight nap, which trust me was a God thing because that does not usually happen.

When I landed I was supposed to look for two people, "Luda and Perla" whom I had never met or even seen pictures of, and they were going to be my ride from the airport. The journey was about to begin for the summer. I could have done some research asked for their pictures, looked them up on Facebook, something in this world of technology, but I didn't. I don't know why, but I didn't - I just trusted God to take care of the process and he did. Luckily my bags showed up when I exited the plane and I walked outside the airport to the arrival station just like I remembered that decade before. There were fewer people traveling with me and no meat with me this time. I was looking around for these two people.

A T-shirt of the organization that I was working for caught my eye before I ever even saw my name on the sign they had so creatively drawn. Immediately Luda was nice enough to take my bags to the car. Perla and I began to introduce ourselves and try and get to know each other as quickly as possible. We knew wanted to be best friends for the summer. I am so glad that friendship has lasted much longer than that. I thought we would be off in a car headed to where we were going to put our stuff for the ten weeks, but I was wrong. Remember I hadn't really done my "what do I need to do when I get there" preparations.

The thing I did not realize was that I was the first to arrive of the three U.S. interns that they would be having for the summer. Prior to that point, I thought I would be the only one from the U.S. who would be joining this staff. That was okay, but something about having the two other girls coming was awesome. We were able to go to the top of the airport and get some food from Joan, who grew to be one of my amazing friends. My perspectives of the airport were changing as I returned, and the people made the airport a joy. Each time I would come to the airport to wait on groups after my initial arrival, I would look for Joan. There were times when she would sit with me and we would just talk about life and people. She would place my order (typically a club sandwich) because this was one of the only times I would have lettuce or sliced deli meat that summer. When it was ready, I would get called by name to come pick it up. At the end of the summer she even saved me bottle caps for a project that I wanted to work on once I returned home.

These airport visits were among one of the few times that I would have fries over the summer and once I discovered their club sandwich, one of the only times I would get a standard United States meal. Even though the prices were steep for these two things, it was worth it. During this initial meeting and eating at the airport, Luda, Perla and I were able to talk and ask the normal questions of what is your favorite food, movie and so on, to get to know each other. By the time the other two girls' flights arrived, I already considered Luda and Perla family, a feeling that still remains. The drive back to the house where we would be staying for a few days was an interesting one. Driving rules in Belize were not the same as at home.

Some images from my first trip came back really fast with speed bumps still in full force, the roads never were without people passing on either side of you, sometimes with cars. Bike being ridden while riders carried weed eaters, fans, family members or all of the above, and your random montage of animals, dogs, snakes, geckos, and the like, passing you. Going to the northern part of the country, which I was not used to, it was fun to see the sights and sounds. The more north you went, the more spread out the areas became, and you came to see the beauty and simplistic nature of this country. After a few days, we would join everyone out on the island for training and our summers of groups coming in and working at churches in the country would begin, I could not have been more excited or more ready for this to happen.

When we met with the staff, I already was challenged to try my Spanish that had not been practiced since my freshman year of college. Let me explain, in college I don't know if it was ever really practiced. In high school we learned the theme song to "Once Upon a Time in Mexico" as part of our homework. So my Spanish at this point would truly become an interesting mix of Creole, and English with an "a" or "o" on the end, or actual Spanish words, but not used correctly. Some of that would change over the course of that summer; however, there would always be an interesting, let's say "flavor" to the words in which I spoke. As I edit this I am back again in Belize. Though the knowledge of the Spanish language is deepening it will never be beautiful. My conjugation stinks, something God uses continuously to make me laugh and be humble all at the same time.

We met for a few days with the staff that I would be working with for the summer, and had our meetings on the rooftop of a hotel that overlooked both sides of the island. It was a sight to be seen. We had time to enjoy meals together, train together, hope, learn, and pray together. It was a time when we could bond before breaking up as our groups came in on different days. Some groups would begin coming earlier than others, so as the week progressed, leaders dispersed from the island to start the summer. The pastors that we were to be ministering to would also meet with us on the island, as we would talk about the later groups that would be coming to visit their villages and the group expectations vs. the church's expectations, and begin to mediate that difference as the summer progressed.

It was amazing to see how inspired the church leaders would get by just coming together and meeting with us and with others that they never had met before. This was truly the body of Christ living and active. Pastors from all over the country were being brought together over a common purpose and passion to reach people and make God known. They were an encouragement not only to the groups from the United States but the other pastors present who were sacrificing some of the same things that they were. It was exciting to see Christ move in this area and people all brought together because other groups wanted to come down and bless each one of them.

After training was over, our work began. Some went to the villages to get things set up, while others were in charge of going back to our host home and getting supplies and helping out there until our groups arrived. During the entire summer, there would not be a day or time when we were all together on the island again. We would see the groups and teams as we would pass their village, at police checkpoints and sometimes running into our host home to grab a supply that we forgotten, get a quick hug from our host mom, or some quick internet usage. We would take a moment and catch each other up on our week and talk about who did the craziest thing - and then out the door we would go again. This was life, and we loved it.

The first group that I was with went to a church in the northern part of the country. This pastor grew to be one of my favorites, even when I was working in another area if I was within five miles of him, I would stop and say hello to him and his family. Let me just describe him for you. He was in his mid to upper 60's with short white hair.

He was small in stature, about 5'5' - 5'6'. He had the personality that could light up a room. Always dressing in a t-shirt and usually jean shorts, his name was Ermilio. He never was without his black, low top Converse shoes. Another item he was never without was his three-wheeled bright neon blue bike. He was a sight to be seen. The group there was to install new tin sheeting on one outside section of their church, to act as a roof for this area over a grassy 12x20 plot of land. This section was where the church had their children's Sunday School section. As we were beginning to work on this project, we were looking to find the best way to get the old tin off.

I remember vividly Ermilio climbing on the roof quicker than anyone I have ever seen with his Chuck Taylor shoes and no ladder. Somehow in two jumps he was up on the top, helping the group out. Then I remember him later pouring concrete in the same shoes and they were covered in concrete. He didn't care, because the group was helping his church, so he was not going to let getting his dirty shoes stop him from helping. I have that picture of his cemented shoes working in the concrete framed in my kitchen. Most people say that it is a weird picture to have framed in my kitchen. Most ask or wonder why it is there. Every time I see this picture it is a reminder to me that it is important to put our best foot forward for God and sometimes that means that we or things we have get messy.

There are so many different analogies, that I could go on and on with this picture and with how God used this man many times in the two different weeks I worked with him and his family. However, for now let me just say he was a significant part of my struggle and left a huge impact on my life. I still talk to his daughter on occasion and make sure to check in with her mom and dad and tell them that I said hello. He challenged me in my faith, my Spanish and my construction skills, reminding me you are never too old to dream another dream.

There were times that tested my leadership and my skill set. I remember one day after looking at a site, I could not deem it worthy to have a group there. It would be one of my initial trips of the summer, and there were too many safety issues, so that the inner mom in me came out. I could not conscientiously be held responsible for a team if we were to work on the roof of that building. This was a building that was all concrete. The sides and floor were simple and smooth, both painted in a white wash color that easily depicted most Belize houses and churches. If we had been working on the inside or on the grounds, that would have been one thing. However, the church needed a roof and pillars on the second story of their building. The roof of the first floor was cemented but not flat. The surface on which they would have to work and set ladders to work on was very rough and jagged with no two spots level. A few different trips and many bug bites and ant bites later, the stories are too numerous to count. There are moments - moments when I felt God in the smallest and the biggest of ways. Moments when I questioned God about what was coming next, and wondered if the next group would fit in with the area that we were going to. One thing remained: He is faithful.

Every time we were at the airport waiting on the next group, there would be butterflies that would well up in my stomach as people would come off the airplane in their green and teal shirts. After just a few weeks of being in the country I was consistently greeted with hugs and huge smiles from different restaurant owners, airport personnel, and water taxi employees. When my dad when back to Belize a year later, he was known as "Elizabeth's dad".

I love this country. There was one group in which I knew almost everyone that was on the trip since it was the second time they had come. There was something about this group. They had smiles that were contagious, and the group members were matchless. I would keep up with them throughout the year and I would check in on their lives and they on mine. Many times I would receive prayers through Facebook about them thinking of trips in Belize, and God placed me on their hearts to pray for that week. I had conversations about cameras, interning and the list goes on and on. I even saw two members of one of my previous groups skiing in West Virginia while chaperoning another youth trip, and it was if I had not missed a day without talking to them. They were and are special.

While their group was in Belize one year, their project was to build the beams of the wall that would eventually hold the roof they hoped to put on the following year. Similar to the roofing project that I previously said no to, this one differed in that it was on the first floor of a building. The group had a contractor who helped with the planning and execution, and the members were prepared and ready to do this type of work upon their arrival. This was a bigger project than I thought and much rebar and cement later, walls and beams were being constructed. We got to the point halfway in the week that the job that was remaining was could only be done by the men in group. The younger children would not be able to lift the five gallon buckets full of concrete up to the people who were standing on ladders and pouring it into the troughs they had made the day before. To be honest, I didn't want to do this, either.

This was a disgusting and very dirty job, but this is how the beams were built in Belize and the men were up for the task. The day approached and all of the troughs had been built and the rebar formed. Now it was time to mix and pour the concrete. So as one group was getting ready to lead Bible school at another location the men stayed back and worked… and worked… and worked. When I went up to check on them and make sure they were drinking enough water, they were covered from head to toe in cement. Yet, they still had their infectious smiles. Leaning against the wall, physically exhausted from the lifting and heat, they were beaming. They saw something being accomplished for someone else and they were more than willing to make it happen. This was a sight that I will never forget. This was one way I saw the men "going away closer".

This group has since gone home and also returned to Belize. They still impact the church that they created the roof for that day. They are still a part of the families' lives that are being changed in that area and each time they come, they create deeper relationships with the ones they know and new relationships with friends and families in the area. They have also been a continuous blessing to me as I have spoken with or seen members of this group over the past years. Their encouraging prayers for me and my ministry wherever I am having been an amazing blessing in my life. One member of this team is currently interning with the same missions group, and seeing his summer unfold brings back the greatest memories.

During this time in Belize, I was also in the heart of my master's program. My degree specifically required an immersion piece since I was an Intercultural Studies major, and this meant that I needed to travel somewhere and experience a country and culture. This could be done in various ways; however, I was very blessed to have this summer spent in Belize not only count in so many ways for my personal growth and development, but also for my professional developments as my master's degree requirements were being met. Among the different aspects that had to be met for this class, we were required to create journals for our professors that showed how our lives were being impacted by others and the experiences we had. I was already a pretty avid travel journaler, but this inspired me to look at the experience in a new and different light. I am fortunate enough to still have those journals tucked away in my divinity school work. I am able to see through these journals the way God was coming closer through social, economic, and spiritual advances that I was proud to witness and in some cases be a part. God was restoring his people through relational experiences.

The summer spent in Belize taught me many things. It taught me how God's grace is amazing, especially when it comes to my Spanish and Creole speaking capabilities, which Luda, would laugh at often. It taught me how amazing and grateful people can be if their hearts are open and how willing they can be to share life with you if you are paying attention. Belize taught me that the sunsets can be just as stunning at the top of a Mayan, ruin in the middle of a rainforest, or in the heat of a soccer field with children running around everywhere. It also taught me about myself, showing me the need to be found over and over again in Christ, in his truth and his grace.

This does not mean that you can or need to be saved more than once, but it is a constant reminder that to be in Christ is to be in his word, with his people, and obeying his leading. Belize taught me two things more than anything: that if He gives me a direction, there is no stopping him and me together. This is why this book and other things in my life have come about. Secondly, he taught me if we can minister and make an impact in one place if led by God, we can minister and make an impact anywhere, regionally or locally.

Belize Aftermath

Coming home was something different for me, for parts of my heart will always be left with the people of Belize and that initial trip. I had no idea how God would mold and direct my paths in the years to come to grow closer to this country that I originally fell in love in.

The entire reentry process I had never heard about. The feelings that well up inside of you when you come back from a trip that challenges your mind, body and soul, and much like how I feel that Post Traumatic Stress Disorder, (PTSD) would be. Though I have never been through this in the military, the correlations that I find between the two are more than not, and I don't take PTSD lightly, I feel there is a huge emotional weight that happens when you truly listen to yourself after a mission, trip especially your first.

There is this feeling when you come back from your first mission trip that I just can't explain. Almost it is this sense of loss, that there is a part of you that you left in the place that you visited that you can never get back. There is this understanding and sometimes unfortunately reality that anyone who did not go with you on the trip can never fully understand what happened to you and why you changed. You were just gone for a week, and it should not be that impactful. Right? Wrong. Those who did share the journey and the trip with you are all at different stages of their faith and walk with Christ. They have a disconnect between what you saw and felt, and how you were moved and changed in those meaningful moments and days. There is a reality that if you go back to the same place and the same country even within the same year that you will be changed. The people you ministered to initially will be changed and things that you hoped and wished for, for nostalgia's sake will never ever be the same again. This does not make your story less valid; just the opposite, more valid because it is a story only you can tell.

Things back home will be different. You will covet the hot water that a shower brings and understand the joys of taking a shower with running water, be it cold or hot. Those amenities are enjoyed by few people. You will quickly see yourself turning off the faucet more, turning out the lights more, and truly enjoying being disconnected from the world. There is this reality that sets in that we have all created our busy nature and only you and I are to blame. I saw the houses and the dirt floors and the tv' s sitting on the ground with the single light bulb that illuminates the house and the raw wiring that was hanging around where the children were playing. There are times when you want to rush in and fix all that. However, one must remember their home and their culture, whether you are down the road or a thousand miles away, are different from our own. A relationship is needed to understand and analyze what is their greatest need (according to them) and then attempt with the power and responsibility that you have been given to fix it according to their customs and cultures if you are able.

A reality hits you somehow almost the instant your plane hits the ground or your car pulls into the driveway. There is this notion that there's so much more work to be done and that you should quit your jobs, your life and your passions, and go make them happen in the foreign country. Though this may become true for some, I find that in my life when I get home and my head hits the pillow for the first time in weeks that I find myself thinking about ways in which I can do locally what I did in a foreign land.

You may have been sincere about the prayers and continue to remember Joseph, Eremilio, Evelyn and others by name at night. A few days after you are home, you may realize you don't know your neighbors down the street, their birthdays, their struggles, or maybe even their names. This is a HUGE disconnect. If we are to "love our neighbor as ourselves" how are we showing that to the ones we literally live beside? While we do such a good job of showing it internationally, we have created a chasm that desperately needs to be fixed at home.

Don't get me wrong - I have always participated in helping locally. From serving food at the homeless shelter, to working on Habitat for Humanity houses, to helping with clothing and food drives, I enjoy it. I enjoy the people and the self sacrificial nature that comes from serving alongside of others that I get to see at home on a more frequent basis than abroad. However, once you come back, there is a change of heart. From the easy and bold nature that you obtain while traveling internationally, you didn't mind about walking up to people and to their houses and telling them that Jesus loves them. Then you followed it with you would be praying for them.

I have found that the relationships that I have had for a long time are often ones where it is hardest to open up for conversations about Jesus and how he is working in your life. We all fear judgment and failure. We find ourselves in between a rock and a hard place situation where if we tell others about Jesus, they can judge and ignore us; but if we don't, then at the final judgment day what difference will we have made? Have we really done all that God wanted us to do?

The more I go on missions abroad, the more I come home looking and anxiously waiting to see how and when God is going to use the situations and conversations that I experienced overseas, a way that only he can do locally.

Costa Rica

During the Advent season, the week prior to Christmas, I went to Costa Rica. This was different for me because I am used to traveling on missions during the summer. It is amazing how we each get in our routines so easily. Waking up at a certain time, brushing our teeth a certain way, having the same thing to eat for breakfast can all quickly become mundane and monotonous. Once I had committed to this December mission trip, different things had to be put into place to make this trip possible. Typically, in the summer all that is required is to take off work and leave the sun to go visit the sun. However, Christmas is different. Working with family schedules, church, work, etc, life was a little chaotic.

I was teaching at the time, and so all of my student's grades had to be put in prior to my leaving, and subs had to be found for the two days that I was going to miss. Also, during that time I was heading a project at church that culminates in a toy store for our campus, and I could not obviously be in two places at once, so I had to find another person who was willing step into this role. I have found over and over again when God wants something to happen, he will make it work. Period. Many times God will leave you in a trail of awe and wonder so you will know that it was only through Him that something has been accomplished. The leader who agreed to lead the toy store outdid herself with taking over the team. Have I mentioned that God is amazing?

Then it came the realization that the week that I would be gone during Christmas would be the week that typically wait to begin my Christmas and my dad's birthday shopping. This meant that I had to be prepared and shop prior to the trip even wrapping some items before I left, (trust me this never happens). I made sure to put names on the presents I wrapped, or I would be rewrapping them, because I could not remember what was in them. So here I was in the midst of the chaos, getting ready for a trip that was to be in December. Every day I was working at multiple jobs - one that I had taken on for the holiday season, was a mess.

There were only a few times that I was able to pause for a moment and reflect on the Advent season. Typically, I was so tired that the reflection became more of a trance and therefore wasn't really a communion with God. During this time, I was able to see how when we do things with God, he is able to orchestrate plans that we never thought possible or even probable. I was able to get my teaching restructured and secure the subs. I was able to get the test printed and the classes ready for my students. With His help, I was able to immediately go from finishing work at one job straight to another and somehow find time to still have my two bible studies and get some sleep in the process. God showed me that when we come together surrounded by his plan, his purpose, and his will, we see something that is amazing and beyond our expectations.

I had been on my phone a ridiculous amount prior to leaving on this trip. The amount of calls that I received and the emails I had to return exceeded almost anything that I can remember. I can handle my phone until a point, and then I reach an unknown limit. There are times when it just needs to fly across the wall and break into a million pieces (though God forbid) because I would then have to pay to get me connected to the world again. What a never ending cycle. God was working in these moments of preparation, because when we embarked on the trip to Costa Rica, my phone was not turned on for five days straight. It may seem strange that this is such a feat, since for some this may be a normal occurrence. I have friends who turn their phone's off just because they don't want to talk to anyone for a few days, and then they resurface to the world and no one thinks anything of it. However, in the technological and ever changing world that we live in, my phone is typically on ready to respond to the next email, text the next person or deal with the next problem. Being able to revert to what it was like prior to the cell phone on this trip was eye-opening.

To see the simplicity in which people lived was a beautiful reminder of how we should commune with God. However harsh we may think their environment is, they have great joy in getting items that we could buy almost every day. The children received watches, not because they needed them to tell time, because time to them didn't matter. They also were not able to read the hands on the watch if it was not digital. What mattered was how that watch, which would become a bracelet when the battery would eventually die, meant it was their personal present that they didn't have to share with someone else. This was a gift that was above and beyond a necessity, but a true gift for them to enjoy. This was worth it. To see a small plastic dump truck, with no electronics or lights, being pulled and raced again and again by Joseph and Jordani was uplifting. They had a pure joy of life.

I witnessed parents taking just as long as their children, and some even longer, in coloring the coloring page they were given with meticulous detail. They would probably use it on a "wall" in their house, if you could even call the sticks that held up the roof a sturdy wall. It was amazing to see how God, both in the big picture and small details, can bring things to our minds when we return. I thought about the simple things over and over: roofs without holes, walls that are more than sticks held together by string, actual doors, let alone locks that make me feel secure. Small pleasures I take for granted over and over again.

It has made a difference, in the fact I have not watched but a few hours of Christmas movies and no other television since I returned. I have taken faster hot showers, even though I know my water tank is capable of handling the hot water. I have eaten the food that was on my plate or prepared by someone else even if it was not the greatest because it was there and others were going without. I have not had anything to drink other than water and occasionally apple juice, because I don't need anything else,

I am not saying that mission trips should bring you back with a cynical and senile perspective that everything needs to be changed and things such as electronics should be thrown to the curb. It is through these technical advances that we can upon return raise awareness and advocacy on many levels, leveraging the resources we already use on a daily basis for a positive action or benefit. I am saying that we need to be aware of our fortune and how we align our passions and resources to fit in with where, when, and how God is leading us both here in our day to day life and abroad. I am not the only one who feels this way. Check out Jeff W's story. He has been on and led many trips, and his life not only has been impacted but changed and transformed by the trips he has taken.

"I have been thinking about your question and for me personally my experiences internationally definitely fuel my passion to serve anywhere God opens a door! I remember my first international trip and how it changed my life, and when I returned home I was convinced that serving here and around the world was God's calling on my life. I began leading trips through my local church, and the Methodist Conference, to West Virginia, disaster relief around the eastern US, Church construction in Alaska, and of course back to Costa Rica. As I began to take others to Costa Rica, I saw the same life change happening in their lives, and the same desire to serve when they returned. Since then it has been my life's goal to expose as many people as I possibly can to the international mission experience! There is just something about getting away from the distractions of our lives, far enough the cell phone won't work, and seeing first hand that everyone in the world doesn't live with the fortune we enjoy every day of our lives. This experience almost always allows God to draw out the servant's heart that He created in each one of us." - Jeff W.

He Came Closer

He did it, as he always does. In the midst of it all, He was there. In the still small voices and the silence, He was in the midst. I love the word "midst". The literal definition of the word from Webster is the "middle area or part of something" or "the condition of being surrounded or beset". This word could not be more accurate. I am sitting here typing as the hair on my head is still wet from the shower that I took right when I got home and the laundry is tumbling in the room down the hall. Yes, I have been traveling again and this time I did not think it was for mission. This time I was with my friends enjoying a short but much needed time away on a cruise. These friends are special, for they have been a part of a Bible study that has been at my house for the past two-and-a-half years. Some are newer to the group, but none are any less important. This was a time when we could just get away and relax void of our phones, internet, and yes, even our computers. Can you tell I like to be away from my phone at points? What a blissful few days this was. I did not have any plans. After I got on the boat, it was rare that I had my phone with me to tell the time and when asked what to do, my typical response was "I am on vacation so I really don't care. I just might sit here all day long."

That is what I was able to do, sit, relax and see the goodness that God has made. I enjoyed His creation in moments that still in their silence seem to beckon me closer. Through the illustrious sunsets, water and people, He has given me a path to mold, shape and guide my journey every step of the way.

As the Dramamine is wearing off after 26 hours my body is beginning to sway as I feel the rhythm of the boat that I was on rocking back and forth. It is crazy to think how this for five days can get you in a motion that when you're back on steady ground it is hard to break. This reminds me of how when we are in rhythm with God, it is hard to get out of that swaying back and forth into his arms of hope, grace, and peace. Now I told you that this was my Bible study group that was on the trip. We did not have anything planned and didn't do a bible study each night, but nightly there was some way in which God worked in and through our day. It was a time to just be in the presence of one another and with God.

There were moments of sheer laughter when I could not pronounce something, or something would come out a combination of two words and I did not mean for it to, like "s'more" for some more. When we would all join together for dinner, being able to take that time and bless the food as each took turns saying the prayer was a memorable experience. Just this brief and normal thing that we do daily took on an entirely new meaning in this context, with people from all over the world surrounding us, at my table, and all around the dining room.

I mentioned at the beginning of this chapter that He came near. I did not expect him to... I was on vacation, not a mission trip. Often God works the most in the times and the places which we do not expect. I have learned to never say "never" when it comes to anything having to do with God. Though no studies were done, and honestly in the moment I may not have seen him working, he came closer.

God was with us when we were in our emergency station. Yes, God is with us in emergencies; however, this was the preparing for an emergency... not a real one. This is the required time that you have to all huddle together in case a "titanic" moment just happens to occur and you need to all leave the ship by following directions. If you think that this would really happen, I beg to strongly and sincerely differ. However, we were sitting awaiting our instructions and two ladies sat down beside me-one from Florida and her friend from Mexico. We shared our names and shared a few words in Spanish and where we had traveled in each other's countries and for a few brief moments I was able to see how God, even for a minute, can put someone or something in your path to make a difference, change your decision about a problem or just to make you smile.

We had had a long day. This early riser had her normal early wake up time and was the first one up most of the days. The long days honestly consisted of doing nothing, (what a concept). So tired from doing nothing, we decided that the hot tub sounded like just the thing to relax us before going to get ready for dinner that night.

There were many people in the hot tub so we had to split up into two groups, one going to one hot tub on the left and the other on the right. We just sat and talked amongst ourselves in small social chatter. Then a few people got out and the water was getting too warm for our bodies. Many of us just began sitting on the edge with our feet in the water. One of the two people who had been sitting beside us the entire time spoke up and asked where we were from. It was at this point that I met John and James. In our typical fashion the response was "above Charlotte," because that usually suffices People not from North Carolina only typically know Charlotte or maybe Raleigh, but not this time they asked for more details again. We find out they were currently living in Greensboro.

As the conversation continued, we begin to ask what each of us did for a living, and I spoke up with my involvement in missions, travel and international students. This started a wonderful conversation. James had formerly lived in Dubai for seven years. Prior to that, he lived in South Africa and London. It was amazing to see how God brings people from all around the world close to us, even when we do not realize it. John, on the other hand, grew up in Florida, meeting his wife there. They moved around from Alabama, then to Greensboro.

They began asking about my involvement in missions and how we all had a passion for helping others. The conversation flowed into speaking about water missions, one of which was, Wine to Water (a great organization that is worth checking out), and also a few other organizations that take water into areas that do not have any. Interest was expressed in taking a mission trip instead of a family vacation, so they could see how they could be a blessing to others. In the moment, I did not realize how much of a blessing these two men were being to me. Preceding me in age by 20 to 30 years, with families of their own they had a heart for mission and a passion for people. They met in an odd circumstance, both at the time working for the same company but in different departments and countries and then became friends close enough to take a cruise together with their families. When asked about who we were here with, we said a Bible study. They were in shock that something like that could and did happen. It was a great moment to see God using our stories to work in each other's lives. It is my prayer that both their families follow through with the idea of a mission trip for their next vacation. I pray that they can be impacted by the love and joy that mission trips bring and they can understand the resources they have when they give their time and attention to something. As the conversation ended, I would not see either one of them or their families again on the boat. However, I am reminded that it is not the quantity of life in which you spend with one that makes a difference, but the quality. I pray that our conversation was just as impactful for them as it was for me.

Another great moment where God came closer on this trip was at the beach. You each understand at least partially my fascination with water and how just like fire I am mesmerized by its enormous nature: strong yet soft; forceful yet gentle, sustaining yet violent. We were at the beach on a day a port, and at this point of the day we had been there for a few hours, enjoying the quietness that was around us. We were some of the first few out on the beach and the other people from the cruise had not discovered this beach yet. After a few hours, it was beginning to get crowded. Not only was the water and tide coming in, but more people were coming out on the beach, for six cruise ships were docked at the same port. Can you imagine the influx in a day of 14,000 to 16,000 people unloading from one dock? This was crazy to me. There was room for chaos and disorder, but there in the midst of it all was God. There were massive amounts of alcohol around, with people both selling and buying. People were walking around cursing and selling drinks, cigars and all the things that tourists many times get themselves trapped into when they travel. People were everywhere. Then families were trying to cram into the middle of all of this nonsense, all for a place on the beach. Behind us came a family, and being so close, I was able to hear a little bit of their conversation. I know eavesdropping is not a good characteristic to have; however, when you can reach out and touch their feet without having to get up because you are so close, somehow I think that falls into a different category.

The family behind us was not your typical family. It included one mother, father, and a baby who was eight months old and adorable. Then there was a cousin and an uncle to the mother of the family. The parents of the mom had both passed away within the past two years and the uncle was basically filling in on the parental, and grandparent duties. He was doing a great job. The baby was just laughing away as he played in the sand, and the parents would come and check on them every once in a while. While I never saw the uncle get up and enjoy the ocean, he just was enjoying time with the family that he had. Then something changed. I had gone for a walk and I came back and the uncle was sitting in the sand now not with the baby but with one of the ladies who roamed the beach asking everyone and anyone if they wanted a bracelet, scarf or their hair braided. I found this kind of odd that she would be wasting her day sitting and talking to this man. Then I heard another woman, who also sold items on the beach come and ask what the lady was doing. Before she could get a word in edgewise the uncle said that she was her Bahamian family and five years ago he had met her on this same beach and they had talked then and shared their stories and became good friends. He held up a picture of the lady sitting beside him from five years earlier and showed it to the woman who had asked the question. The picture depicted something that I will never forget.

The two of them were sitting in the sand, not knowing if and when they would ever see each other, but reliving the stories that they shared with others, talking about growing families and sharing new stories with one another. It was a moment where the "good music" is played in the movies. The climax is reached when the friends are reunited after not knowing if they are ever going to see each other again. Asking serious questions about each other's health and wellbeing they were truly investing in each other in a way I could see. I could see on the woman's face that uncle would provide encouragement for the many days, months and years to come. As the niece and her family walked back up to the seats, he introduced each one of them to the woman sharing a slight bit of her story, but not forgetting that she was still there to encourage. The time that he took out of his day to meet her where she was, was something miraculous. It was something that could not be canned, or pickled or savored for later. It was something that only that moment and that time would handle. I do not know how long they stayed talking, for they were still there when I left and I do not know if the woman continued to work after they finished, because she had missed hours of potential income. All I know is for that brief but wonderful moment, God was in our midst, in the form of brotherly love without borders and no sense of time, but just there walking alongside each one of us.

While we were on the beach, right before we left, I went for a walk to throw away my trash from lunch, I was walking to the trash can when I passed by a woman in a wheelchair and a guy on his knees behind the chair in the sand. I did not realize what was going on but I watched for a minute. These two were both Bahamian and they were either family or close friends. The guy was pulling two levers on the back of the wheelchair that lowered and raised the back of the chair, causing the woman to be able to sit up straight or to lie down flat. At first, I believe, he was doing this for her exercise, because slowly he would raise up the chair and then bring it down. As time passed he stopped this motion and after talking to her, lowered the chair to just the right position so she could lie in the chair in the sun while he attempted to sell trinkets in his makeshift tent on the beach. Every so often he would go over to her and check on her and see if she needed to be repositioned, but then they would just talk back and forth as the day progressed. This was God showing me love, and going away closer.

The weather on the cruise was amazing. Typically, you have that one day when it is just rainy and nasty, but this was not the case. There was an amazing day each time we woke up in the morning. The wind was blowing (sometimes strong), but the sun was shining and it reminded each of us to be still and know that he is God. We had one full day that we spent on the boat at sea during the day. This was great. Though windy the sky was bright and it brought hope that vacation could go on forever, (even though the reality would soon hit us). With the girls each reading their books and the guys napping in the sun, something of peace surrounded these moments. There were times when the right song would come on and each of us would just stop everything and sing the lyrics. Then the times when we each would feel a strong rock in the boat and look at each other, making sure it wasn't just us. These were fun moments. Then as all of this was occurring, Andrew pointed up to the sky which had been just full of a light blue expanse with clouds here and there. To the right of the sun was a patch, looking almost like a patch for a pair of pants. However, this was not an ordinary patch. This was a rainbow, not arched or one sided or even long but a square space where the light reflected off the sky in just the correct manner that we saw a rainbow without any rain. I think that sometimes God just likes to show off and see how much he can make us smile when he has the "Look what I can do moments". This was one of those. Looking at the rainbow full of colors, we could not replicate but God says, wait a minute and see my splendor, my majesty, my radiances, without you doing anything for me. God is a glorious God who wants us closer.

Day after day after day the night sky would be painted in an array of colors that would take your breath away. One night, waiting for a few to finish up getting ready for dinner, we had the curtains open in our room and the sun was shining in as it descended over the edge of the horizon. With every minute of its descent, the layers of colors just seemed to keep coating the sky. There was a new canvas and piece of art with each blink of the eye. The sky radiated with reds, pinks, purples, and oranges, cascading over the sea as if it were made solely and completely for that mere second of time. I honestly believe it was. With each minute I could not take my eyes off of the splendor that lay just outside my window. Making my way closer for a better view, I saw the seas become darker and the texture of the sky left me breathless. There was something about this moment, just like many other sunsets, that no matter how many angles or ways in which you take a picture this moment, this time, was made for you to breath in, and savor it for that moment. Then you can release so something else wonderful can be created. This moment was stunning. As I just sat there watching the sky melt off the face of the horizon, I could not help but see how he was showing me how close he always is. The song "and he walks with me and he talks with me and he tells me I am his own" could not have rung more true in my ears. My God, my very own, unexplainable, incomprehensible, unwavering God talking to me, walking with me, telling me that I am his beloved. What a moment. The sky faded into the night and the time for dinner came, but the moment that God and I shared together was our own, our way of going closer.

Part 2

I was reading a book loaned to me by my best friend the other day and something within it spoke to me. As I was reading I came across a phrase I have not thought about before: "I'm going to abandon my dream but not my god."[13] This phrase got me to thinking. I believe 100 percent that God gives us the desires of our heart. However, I believe 100 percent that God does not give us what we believe our desires are, but what he sees deep down we truly desire. To me this is two vastly different things. There are many times in life when I have stated or said that I truly desired something, and in the moment I feel as if God did not grant this request - that somehow he was void of that time or situation. God is never void or apart from you. God may not be talking, or He may be waiting on you to make the next move. God is never apart from you. Psalm 37:4 declares "Take delight in the LORD, and he will give you the desires of your heart." Always, and I mean always looking back with the right perspective I have seen that God in his infinite wisdom granted even my strange requests to meet the needs I had at that time. They were desires filled completely by him.

I am a huge bucket list fan. Before the movie came out, I was coming back from the Passion Conference in Atlanta on a tour bus and we had a long ride. I sat down beside, Lane, one of the friends I had met that weekend, and we began discussing bucket lists. At this point I did not have a written bucket list. This was all about to change. There were things in my head that were ideas of places and events that I wanted to experience, but also things I wanted to experience with certain people. Lane got me thinking about the need to write all of these things down, not only to get them on paper and to see if they could become a reality, but to see if they were really desires or just random things I wanted to accomplish. I accepted a bet from Lane to see who could have the most things on their bucket list. I wanted to write down what I wanted to do, so I could look back and remember it. So 524 things on a list later and still growing mind you, my bucket list is now ready to be used and accomplished. Looking

---

[13] (Wilson, 31).

back there are a few overlaps, but most of them are as diverse as the sunsets that God paints in the sky, never two alike. I typed up the list and printed it out and challenged my roommate to create one also. She said she would live through mine and I am excited to say that each year when we go through the list to check off what we have done the previous year, there are always at least two or three things that God has allowed us to experience together.

I've included this story to say I have a list of things which I want to accomplish. Some may seem trivial, such as going to eat at a certain restaurant. Others include traveling to places or meeting specific people. Time and time again, I have seen God use this list in ways that I never thought possible. God has spoken to me through this list. While I was on mission trips or serving locally, God has fulfilled my desires which he gave me prior to creation. This has inspired me to have a flame sparked by his power, working in and through people, places, and things which I never thought possible or imaginable. I have also seen how sometimes, if I allowed myself, this list could carry me away from God's plan for my life and become a self-seeking wannabe list of things that have to be done to make me complete.

One of the things on my list was to light a paper lantern and release it. You may think, well, you could have done that, just order one off line and then release it and you could check it off you list. However, I believe that the list is more important and more revealing when things happen at times you do not expect them. Granted if at some point this would mean that I would have to travel to the festival of lights in Thailand, then I would not be opposed, but I try and leave things to where God can open the doors and not me. Things work out so much grander that way.

What I didn't mention about Costa Rica was it was on my bucket list. Originally thinking I was going to Burundi, Africa, the summer before Costa Rica was not even on my radar. After Africa fell through because of timing and signups, God seemed to manifest this Costa Rica trip. To make it even more special, Africa was on my bucket list also. So God, out of one plan falling through, orchestrated another plan that would yet again open my eyes to serve, and fulfill another desire. While we were in Costa Rica we were missing someone very close to our mission. I saved this story for now because God moved through Costa Rica, my bucket list and Jeff Ward whose thoughts you read earlier, to make this possible. Our trip leader had been diagnosed previously that month with leukemia, and while we were in Costa Rica, he was undergoing treatment options for this brutal disease. We were having our devotionals one night towards the end of the week. The sky was clear and we were wrapping everything up. One of the other leaders of our group said "I think now would be a great time to honor Jeff for the time and effort he put into this trip and earlier trips to Costa Rica. She declared it was something to remember and to pray for him.

She went into her room and came out with nothing other than a paper lantern. At this moment, I almost lost it, breaking down and knowing that only God knew that I wanted to release a paper lantern. Only he knew how special it would be to release it for Jeff. So there we all stood in the middle of camp, lighting the lantern, holding hands and praying together for the mission, the safety, and the health of all that were involved. Those moments of silent reverence will always be captured in my mind and heart, knowing that God hears our cries, and he knows our names. It made me realize how great and heavenly he truly is. (Psalm 34:17, "The righteous cry out, and the LORD hears them; he delivers them from all their troubles.") We released the lantern and allowed it to drift up into the sky as if once it reached a certain height, it was captured by the love of God and held in his arms. As we were all silent, watching it float away, we at that moment became a part of something greater than I could ever imagine. We became even more a part of the team than we were before. We became connected with those who were not with us and ever more connected to a God that is ever present. This is how many times the bucket list allows me a myriad of ways and opportunities to go away and come closer.

I think this is what the initial quote of this chapter was talking about when it said that we need to abandon our dream for God. This means we have to be willing to give up our timing and maybe a few of our dreams in order for God to come in and work in our lives and create the dreams and desires that he has truly given us. Being willing to let go of our prerogatives might just be the very thing that is keeping us from going away closer. How is God using the desires of our hearts to make his kingdom come and our eyes be open to his majesty? Go away closer requires us to think outside of the norm, out of the box, away from the principle that we have all that we need and more toward the principle that we need to leverage what we have to our greatest ability. This is a huge asset and requirement when we see God moving and working in our lives. This is where our hearts and stories from international missions turn and allow us to share, create, live and thrive locally by partnering with others who have hopes, dreams, visions, for the world around us and the world at our home, work, and school doorsteps.

I share these stories with you for a few reasons. One is to open up my journey so that you can walk with me. It is so neat to see how God uses us differently and in ways in which we never expect. Many times I have been silent about those ways. Mission trips and the return process are two very distinct ways in which God shows me his love, his compassion and his passion for us to be in community and relationship with others. Returning is so hard if you don't know where to turn.

It is through mission work that I come home with a new direction, a new sense of calling, and a new passion for what he has brought me here to do. I am not saying that you will have the same call to mission work that I do and I pray honestly that you don't. My story is my own and God is such a big and mysterious God that he is writing a story for you that is uniquely your own. However, in whatever that he calls you to do, I pray that you listen intently to his passion, the purpose he has placed in your life, and the ways in which he is calling you to live in obedience to him.

From these stories I have gained some amazing friendships, networks and seen some wonderful things happen for his kingdom and just in general. I have seen children being born, lives being saved, water brought to people who did not have it, roofs being fixed when they had been leaking and shoes being given to children who have never had a new gift of their own. These moments are something that cannot be taken away from me, moments in which God displays his infinite grace and provision. I share moments which will highlight my ministry moving forward. These moments call me to something greater when returning home. They call me to look for the little things that will make a difference in the lives of others. They call me to work with organizations that prior to trips I had never even thought to look for, nor known they existed, even though they may have been a mile from my house. They have called me to step out of my comfort zone to see the world in which I typically live in a new light and through a new lens of aligning myself both while at home or abroad to live out God's call and mission in my life.

I hope you pay attention to the ways God has called me to work at home, and the ways he has brought other people for me to travel and experience life with as I search for His grace in the middle of the mundane. My prayer for these stories is the same as my previous prayer about the mission trips - that you will not hope that my journey becomes your journey but that you will rest in knowing that God's journey is the best journey. He has a specific and beautiful, though at sometimes hard, journey that is awaiting you. Trust me and more importantly, trust God, that it will be worth it.

We do not have to travel far to make "going away closer" a reality.

Impact

Luxury to me is not about buying expensive things but about living in a way where you appreciate things.

- Oscar De La Renta.

I have been blessed more than I can count and there are times when the comparison monster comes out to play in my life just like he does in anyone else's life. This time, though, it is different. The monster does not come out when people have certain clothes, bags, or jewelry, because the reality of my actually keeping it nice is similar to the reality of my being willing to pay for nice things (virtually non-existent). I am cheap. I have had to learn the difference between investing in something that over a period of time I will get my money's worth out of it, versus just spending money on something that I don't really need because it is the current trend or status of the day.

The traveling to different countries and dealing with locals in various socioeconomic statuses has helped me to realize more and more, it is not what you have, but what you do with what you are given that makes the biggest difference. I have seen it time and time again. The people with the least are often the ones who are the most willing to share what they have, because they know what it is like to be without. It amazes me how God says this will happen over and over, and how the story of the widow's mite comes into play here. It is not the quality that you give, but the motive behind your giving. Your giving should be so much that it limits you from doing some things that you want. If it has been a while since you have heard the story of the widow's mite, or you have never heard it at all, let me refresh your memory.

Found in both Luke 21 and Mark 12, this story is very short but very impactful. We see that Jesus is at the temple watching people place their offerings in the treasury. This action was something that was not uncommon, just like the offering boxes, bags, or plates that we have in our churches today. Yet something was different about this story. There is a woman who is in the temple, and she is a widow.

Socioeconomically at this time, this lady had two things that were going against her. One was that she was a woman, someone who was socially not as powerful as men, and two, that she was a widow. Her husband, now deceased, would have been the breadwinner of the family. Typically, in those times the widows were seen as hassles or financial burdens to families, because they did not have the money or income that would be necessary to support their livelihood. This is not what Jesus was watching. He watched intently with his loving eyes the motives behind her offering- two small copper coins which would be less than a penny in value.

This impressed Jesus so much that he called his disciples to him to tell them of what he witnessed, but he didn't stop there. Jesus proceeded to offer the disciples an insight into the relationship that the women had with her faith. Jesus stated while others gave out of their surplus, or their wealth, she gave out of her poverty or her lack. We have all felt a time or maybe are currently withstanding a time where we are in one of life's lacks. The finances are tight, the job is lost or hopeless, the family ties are severed or about to be and life just seems famished, malnourished, in poverty. Within all of this poverty that we face, we have the ability to exude joy, to spread love, to give with pure motives rather than ill-intent. We have the capability to see that others may have it worse than us, or that we can give someone something that we have an abundance of, not because we are looking for some handout from another person, or recognition that we did something well, but because we are motivated by matters of the heart. We are motivated by love, by Christ and his death and resurrection. When this perspective is in our minds, circumstances change. When this is how we feel, grace is sufficient; when this is our mindset, we are set on things eternal, not things of this world. When we use our resources wisely, it is amazing how creative we can be with the small things to make money go further than we ever expected, and put things into perspective.

When I would travel, originally I would always try to buy gifts for each person that I held near and dear and bring them something back. Though this is not a bad thing, I found that if they were not for a specific birthday or holiday, this process did not really work well for me. I am not saying that we should not bring back things for people, and this is not an anti-souvenir rant. However, I am saying I discovered many times while I was traveling I was focused so on finding something for everyone that often I lost sight of the places where I was and missed some amazing opportunities. I found when I was so fixated on who I had left to buy for, I forgot to take in the beauty of the country, the people, and the culture. My blinders became this built-in blocker until every person on my list was complete. It was then when I realized something needed to change.

An amazing quote from Oscar Wilde states "everything in moderation including moderation." This stuck with me and is a great reminder that even when we are looking for one thing or another we need to make sure that we can be interrupted by the spirit if he chooses. This will allow God to move and work in ways that we might never be able to see again. Be also mindful of the customs of the culture that you are going to. Do they tip? Are they used to getting a certain type of fee? Is one thing an insult vs. one thing a compliment. You can't know all the rules and customs of a foreign area or even a local neighborhood. Don't be afraid to ask what is customary for this time and this place, and the role you should play.

Many people question why I have paid money to travel to places to go work on missions and not to "experience the country." I have had to argue (politely) on many different occasions that I find the argument to be just the opposite. I would argue that it is only when you go and work within the country, if only for a week, and truly interact with the locals, that you are truly experiencing the country. I have seen so many people over and over again buy tickets to places (me included) and go and see the sights, and get some amazing pictures and see some amazing things... the Colosseum, the Eiffel tower, etc. I have been many places, sometimes only for the day, and the sights combined with the people, heritage, history, and stories are what make the experience meaningful. Without the full experience in the culture, the area seems distant; the context seems futile; and the drive for passion seems remote. Yet when you combine a guide who loves the habitat his country has been blessed with ruins or artifacts that no one can replicate, history that has been built upon foundation after foundation, and personal stories only then is the circle complete with the country's true beauty and potential.

It is through the people that you find out their mentality. You find out their names, their stories and even their greatest fears and dreams. From this knowledge, you can create a cultural identity that then can be used when speaking of the country is mindset and demeanor. I am not saying that if you talk to one person within the country, they speak for the entire country. What I am saying is most of the beauty that God created comes from being in relationship with people and understanding and listening to their hopes and desires. He wants this beauty when we have a relationship with him. He wants us to know his story, his history, his joy, of relationships, hopes, forgiveness, and his unending love-because He himself is love. Even though God already knows, he wants us to tell him our hopes, desires, stories, joys, and fears. He wants this constant communion. He wants us to invest in relationships with his sons and daughters to show them his kingdom and his glory, and then to share it with others. His love for us is crazy, wild, extravagant, and intimate. The scenery can tell the story for only so long. The mountains can be breathtaking, the volcanos astounding, the rapids so loud that you can't even think, and the water so blue that you question if there is ever pollution anywhere in the sea. You question why on earth someone would jeopardize this stunning creation. Those memories no matter how great they are, often fade. Pictures of these places can and will not do them justice. They do not have a heartbeat, a soul or an eternal purpose. These places too, will pass away. Without someone standing in the picture, they are almost lost and compartmentalized from our daily lives. They become not just something we experienced once, but something that truly changed us forever.

I have been to some amazing sites, and I have seen some amazing things. One of them was the sun as it was setting on the side of the Roman Colosseum, and for that brief moment everything around the city seemed to pause and breathe over generations past, present, and future. It was a breathtaking sight.

I have seen the Swiss Alps with snow at their peaks, and rafted in their freezing rivers that literally take your breath away because the water is so cold. I have been to the roaring center of where the falls break at Niagara Falls, where you are feeling the mist and sense the strength and power and see what water is truly capable of. I have seen the amazing Twin Towers prior to 9/11 and the strength they displayed, and walked in the Empire State building. The list can continue on and on, and so many books are dedicated to just that… showing and describing the sights and sounds of one location after another and another in hopes that either you will feel like you have been there or you will get such a sensation that you will pay your money to go and see these places for yourself.

I love these places. I love what they mean, the height of an empire, the demise of an era, the strength of nature, man's ability to create and build yet-at each of these locations, I remember not just the sights alone. I remember the moments, who I was with, the times and conversations that I treasured as I shared in viewing some of God's most amazing creations. I go away closer. I then always come home. The sights the sounds, my bed, my pillow, something ingrained in me brings me back. My relationships, my friends, my family, all together encourage. love, support, and spur me on towards Christ and sharing his gospel. I need this "home base". We see in scripture where Jesus says to one follow me, don't even bury your father but follow me. To me initially this seemed harsh, knowing the family base that I have and leaving it with the duties undone. Christ is looking at this through a lens of priorities. Is your family a higher priority thin Christ? Is your job keeping you from him? Is your school work etc.? If so, this is saying to completely disregard those things to allow Christ to regain his rightful place, where he needs to be.

How do the things that we surround ourselves with often entangle us into a lifestyle of comfort and spiritual stagnation? When we do not listen to how, when, and where God calls us to go, we end up in places we never thought possible. Our story isn't shared, and to be honest, our spiritual growth is stunted.

Closer

Coming Back Difference

Our lives begin to end the day we become silent about things that matter.

- Dr. Martin Luther King Jr.

While life eventually goes back to normal, you don't have to.

-Anonymous

I do not understand the mystery of grace, only that it meets us where we are but does not leave us where it found us.

- Anne Lamott

So coming back makes a difference in our lives here but how do we display that difference? Sure we can tell people about our trips and maybe even show a few photos. If you are like me, no one in their right mind would take time to look at all of the photos you took, other than your parents. The photos and the stories go only so far. How can we make a difference in the lives of others at home once we have come back from the trip? I have found that this can be done in different ways. One of the easiest ways that I have found is partnering up with people in your areas who are already doing something really well. Why start something new and go through all that trouble and red tape if you can take just a few more minutes and find something similar to what you are doing and partner with them? This will not only add you as an asset to their team, but it relieves you from the responsibility that you are in charge of that organization. God may call you to be in charge one day, but by partnering, you get to view life of an organization from an insider's perspective and give feedback when necessary.

We may not realize it, but each place we go, if we are closely listening, pulls one heart-string or another. There are times when on location I have been called to start supporting one non-profit and then times when I have been called to pray for a different non-profit organization. God stirs in ways we can't explain but in ways that create waves of effect if we allow them to do so. People come back from mission trips with all kinds of different passions. During this section we see how different experiences have called people to be more involved in general, and then for others caused them to begin championing and carrying a weight of a cause that they at one point never even knew existed. For we are all once blind and then we see; and what an amazing grace that truly is. I hope that the stories that are shared below-not just mine but those of people I have been blessed to friends and brothers and sisters in Christ-inspire you to serve in ways that you never thought possible. We do not have to go across the world to see the world. It is at our doorstep and all we have to do is to be willing to take our blinders off and walk outside to see where God is calling us.

I have been blessed for the past few years to serve in outreach at my church. This service has brought me more joy than any other one thing that I can remember. Though there have been times when it was too much - I wanted to give up or something didn't go according to my plan-I have never not seen God work in and through this outlet of ministry. I have had the opportunity to work with some amazing people that already are doing wonderful things in my local community. I have had meetings with people to set up events when normally it would take a while to get in touch with them. I have seen time and time again God work through the people that serve alongside of me, encouraging others, praying for others and ministering to others when it was not cool to do so. It was taking up their precious time, or people may have seen it as unnecessary. It is through these conversations and moments that I have seen God's beautiful handiwork. Through one of our events, we get the opportunity to serve gifts at Christmas to families who have had a hard year. Using a ticket distributed through our partner organizations, families are allowed to come in and shop for their children, who may not otherwise get a gift that Christmas. The stories that come from moments like these are astounding. The families that remain year after year because they entered the door for the first time one broken and lonely Christmas always warm my heart.

The local ministry partnerships that have been created are some of the best relationships. I love being able to lend a hand to others when they need it and have the action reciprocated when necessary. It is through these partnerships that I have been privileged to witness and hear some amazing stories. I have seen lives changed eternally (the biggest goal that you want any outreach to have). I have seen people become friends and even closer family. It is a pure joy when I am walking in a grocery store and all of the sudden a student comes and runs up to me from one of the summer programs and I get a huge hug and am asked sincerely how I am doing and what I am up to.

The stories go on from the countless times that I have been in an outreach shirt working around town, but especially at the gym, and get asked about something that is coming up at the church and have the chance to tell them about it. Many times I get "You're the girl that does outreach, right?" This is followed by some statement or question about a program or event. One time I had just set down my stuff and was about to start an abs class at the gym, and let me say my confidence level for this class is never that high, so I sat down and immediately the lady to my left asked me that exact question. As I answered with a confused yes, I then recognized her from one of our programs. She would make and bring sandwiches and drop them off at our morning and evening drop sites for the meals we were feeding the community. We started talking about church and I found out she has a daughter about my age, and invited her to ladies' our life group. The stories never get old and God will always put opportunities in front of you to watch and follow if you only take that brief moment to listen and try to hear what is up. Clarity is not something that He gives me on a regular basis; however, He gives me a gut feeling and when that instinct goes off, I know not to disregard and to obey whatever and however it is telling me to move and to act.

One of my favorite times was when I was with friends at K&W. Now if you know me well enough, you know that this is not one of my favorite places to eat. I am not a huge buffet person, even though they serve the food to you, and honestly I don't really like restaurants that serve "home cooking" except for Cracker Barrel. Now hear me out before you completely ban me. My mom is an incredible cook and if you have ever had one of her pound cakes, you would understand where I am coming from. That fact, compounded with the fact that most home cooking consists of casseroles, limits almost to nonexistence the times I go to K&W.

My friend was in town and she wanted to go there, so we went (the things you do for family). While in line, I saw a few people I knew, talked to them as we meandered around to where we were supposed to pick up our food. Then as we went through the line, I spotted a friend from church. She was new to our church at this point and I had met her over the summer as we had our summer lunch program. She was very hesitant to accept sandwiches on the first day, we slowly began to have conversations and talk about life. Shortly afterward she began coming to church and to my life group. So as we approached the end of the line, she spotted me. I smiled really big and waved to her and could hear even in the distance her talking to her co-workers about "these are my church friends; I go to church with them". The smile on her face made mine triple in size because the impact that the church had had on her life and the impact she had on mine will be someone that I will always cherish. These are the moments that make serving locally matter. These personal relationships, just like our personal relationship with Jesus, is what makes life interesting, empowering, inspiring, and refreshing. In the mundane and midst of life, God is always there.

It is my prayer that through the hope and stories of my mission field experience you will be led to go on a trip or support someone who is going financially and/or in prayer as God is at work in and amongst all of the world. There will be times when they will be tested in their faith, hope and purpose, but I pray that you can be the encouragement that they need to hold fast to the promises that God tells us to go into all the world (here and abroad) and preach his name to all people, declaring his goodness, faithfulness, and hope in the darkest of places. Each of us has a little light inside of us, and I pray that we all help each other shine.

Go Away Closer Accounts

I have traveled with and met so many people who have felt this same call to missions not long term living abroad in the traditional sense, but multiple times short term. It is amazing to hear their response and see their immediate smiles when you talk to them about where they went and what they did while they were there. They may mention who they were able to work with and might even mention how many were saved and the experience that happened one afternoon when they least expected it. However, they will always mention how the mission trip changed them, and most of the time mention how it pushed them to make a difference when they returned.

These are just a few accounts of how many have gone and are going away closer...

Many who go on missions trips get asked the question, often multiple times, why go globally when you can go locally right here? I agree there are opportunities that are all around us wherever we are. However, many times we are faced with the "rut" mentality where we are stuck in our status quo and can't seem to reinvent the wheel and put actions behind our words and do the work that needs to be done where we are locally. This is why mission trips are so important. They bring us to an awareness that we are not alone in the struggle but also that we have and are capable of doing work where we are. I follow many people on Instagram many of them are non-profits.

I love the encouragement that comes from their images that are posted often on a daily basis or even more frequently. Sometimes this can take me away from the here and now and I remain focused on my phone rather than doing work that I need to be doing, but many times it offers me the encouragement that I need in one picture because "a picture is worth a 1,000 words" and these pictures speak volumes into my life. One day Samaritan's Feet (a non-profit based out of Charlotte which collects and distributes shoes to those who need them both locally and abroad) posted a picture of a group of Africans who were playing pool on a table that they had made. I stared at this picture at first in disbelief at how they could play pool on such a table. Then like many times when you stare at something long enough, your perspective changes and I was amazed by the ingenuity of the group.

The table, unlike the green felt top that we are used to, was made of mud caked on top of sticks that were laid horizontally. The sides were piled higher with areas just like our tables that had holes for the balls to drop down into. There were smaller balls and two larger mud balls that they were hitting with a carved stick with a blunt tip end. There was an amazing amount of grace that was in this picture, but underneath the grace was the simplicity of nature, the joy of the divine and the hope of the future that their situations would not limit their goals or even their outlook on life. I was astounded by this grace, this hope, this love in the midst of it all. Yet I was humbled by the times that I get so bent out of shape because of something which was made for a specific purpose or plan did not work and I had to improvise. Though I am most of the time good at coming up with a solution to the problems when I am with or leading groups, I let little things that would not bother me in leading bother me personally. Let's look how Samaritan's Feet inspired another person to go, but then come back and serve missionally at home.

Chris P.

"Before I went on my first mission trip in 2012 to Burundi, Africa with Samaritan's Feet and a group from my church. I have always been involved with helping others locally - either through my job as a social worker or as a volunteer with community agencies. This was my first opportunity to do missions outside my own community. I had an incredible and life changing experience while I was in Burundi. To see the level of poverty and the challenges they face on a daily basis and at the same time to see the pure joy and happiness in their lives was a life lesson I will never forget. While I did have the opportunity to support and encourage the people of Burundi, I really do feel like I got more out of this trip than I was able to offer them. When I came back home I realized that I can probably make a bigger difference in someone's life right here in my own backyard - where I speak their language, understand the culture and the challenges they face, and most importantly be able to be involved in an ongoing relationship. I think international mission trips offer a wonderful way for us to all see that we are a part of God's family all over the world and to see how incredibly blessed we are here in the US. I just realized for myself that God was leading me towards work here at home. Within the following year, God had placed the perfect job in my path to work with those who need support and encouragement right in my own community."

Though a different person, time and place God calls us to places all across the globe impacting our lives but also the lives of others. He shapes our realities and inspires us to create change along the way.

Hannah R.

It was January of '06 when I knew God had placed a call to ministry on my life. I may have only been a high school student at the time with no knowledge of what a career in missions would look like, but I resolved to be obedient to the Lord. Almost a decade later I am still discerning the call and walking in the Spirit daily to the best of my ability. In the years between high school and present day, I have explored many avenues of missions and ministry, both locally and abroad.

My undergraduate and graduate degrees focused on studying the Word, learning about missions strategies and developing intercultural communication skills. I took weeklong trips to Guatemala and Germany during college, then after graduation I headed out on an 11-month journey touching base in 11 countries. When I came home I spent 6 months serving the youth group at my home church, then took off again for more studies and a summer stint in Peru.

International travel and missionary work have been woven into the most recent years of my life in significant ways. As I reflect on the work that my teammates and I did internationally, I realize that those experiences have helped me to better understand and recognize the beauty of God and His purposes for His people, as well as equipping me to serve my home community and church more effectively. In Kenya we prayed for the sick, preached the Word, visited the lonely, invited neighbors to church, shared the gospel, laughed with children, danced with worshippers, and followed Jesus wherever he led us. Today, as I live in the little town of Statesville, North Carolina, I still gather with fellow believers to pray for the sick. Each Sunday we come together to hear the Word preached. I enjoy visiting and spending time with new friends and inviting my neighbors to church. There are still opportunities to share the gospel and laugh with children each week in Good News Club at the local elementary school. As far as dancing goes…well, I attend a Southern Baptist church, but I do occasionally attempt a nice sway/rocking motion with a lifted hand or two (And you better believe I have some good dancing worship in my car when I'm riding solo!)

There were several countries where I had the opportunity to meet with some amazing women, both young and old, and remind them of their value and beauty in the sight of God (the only One whose opinion truly matters). At home, I have the same opportunities to encourage ladies and show them that their true worth and identity comes from Christ.

Traveling internationally is always an adventure. There are new sights, smells, sounds and surprises around every corner. People may not look like you, speak the same language or have the same customs and cultures. Everything from food preparation to the method of doing laundry could be completely foreign to the mindset you've always known. Church services may vary in length and style; worship and prayer may be expressed in new ways. **Still, one thing remains the same – God's glory and his love for his people.**

Spending time abroad has enriched my view of God by opening my eyes to the beauty and diversity among the nations and cultures, along with the unity found in the Christian Church as a whole. I have followed Jesus down the dirt roads of Rwanda and it has given me confidence to follow Him down the paved roads of neighborhoods in my hometown. The Spirit encouraged me to sing and dance in worship with international believers and now I look forward to praying and worshipping with my fellow church members.

Until very recently, I viewed my call as a missionary as a very rigid course that would most likely result in living overseas long-term. As

I treasure my past international experiences and plan to continue to learn about culture and communication, **I find that I am no longer choosing to define myself as a "missionary," but rather how the Father sees me as "beloved daughter of God."** If the Lord leads me to the other side of the world or to a small town in the States, I want to be faithful to serve Him. People are people, regardless of where they live, their age, color or social status. And all people have a great need for Jesus. If we know Him, it is our mission to introduce Him to everyone we meet.

I love what Hannah states that "one thing remains the same- God's glory and his love for his people". We see that his love never fails for each one of us, and we are not called to be confined to a box or a stereotype, because we are Christians, we are called to be Christ-like in a world that is Christ-less and there will be varying tasks to which God will call each one of us. It is our job to respond, not to be tied down to the idea or role in which society places us.

What will your response be?

Have you ever imagined life without one of your senses? I am very fortunate that I have all five of my senses (most of the time). Some would say that I selectively turn certain senses off when I deem it necessary; however, most of the time they are fully functional. This is not the case for everyone. There are people who do not have all their senses and they function in life in a completely different way. The ways that they go about their daily routine is different from how others do. It is not bad; it is just different. If you have ever seen any of the YouTube videos that show a person hearing for the first time, it is something incredible to watch. Usually the video starts awkwardly as the nurse or doctor checks the specs of the hearing device and the equipment, then they begin the testing process. This is where you see the transition as the nerves of the patient begin to change and all of the sudden for the first time they begin to hear noises sometimes nothing that really makes sense, and then they begin to translate what these noises mean.

There is a smile that comes over their face. It is not just the turn of their lips upward but literally their entire face is smiling. This is the good part of the video. However, typically there is something that moves you emotionally even further. While they are testing, many times there is a loved one that is in the room. This loved one begins to speak and the first few words that are spoken to their special someone translates worlds. The tears began to flow and for the first time in their life, they hear the voice of someone who accepted them when they did not hear. This is a beautiful picture. This typically brings me to tears as there is a much anticipated reunion with a sense that was not there or was damaged and is now restored. Our relationship with God is much like this. He loves us despite our differences, our self-imposed issues, and our brokenness. He loves us in the middle of our mess and over and over again, he is there to listen, to speak to us when we are just able to hear for the first time, or to be there when we realize that our God-given gift is something that we have had a passion for our entire life but never even realized. It is amazing to see how and where God works.

Check out these stories:

Donna S.

"I have been on several mission trips, but my first trip will always be near and dear to my heart because that's the trip that gave me a new set of eyes. I had been a Christ follower for many years before I stepped out and took my first trip. Back then, I remember thinking you had to be super spiritual, recite and know scripture, and have all the answers to life's questions to represent Christ in another country. Ordinary people like me didn't go on mission trips. Obstacles like finances and language barriers were just more reasons why this Southern girl wouldn't make it to the other side of the Mason-Dixon line. Anyway, I wasn't married. Only couples went on missions. Right? So when a friend of mine asked me to pray about going to Thailand, you can imagine the mental and emotional obstacles I faced. Because a mission trip was beyond my capacity, I moved forward like it was someone else going on the trip. It was only later when the ball was rolling and I was physically getting my passport and shots that I was faced with the reality of my actions. I was going to go on a missions trip!

I spent a month and a half over in Thailand ministering to high school and college students. We made friends, shared the gospel and led Bible studies with Thai students that summer. I came home with funny and exciting stories like the time a toilet fell through the ceiling onto my bed, surrendering my life to a tuk tuk, and shopping on a canal while floating in a boat. I experienced the typical language and cultural barrier, hot and spicy food beyond my taste, squatting instead of sitting, and cultural shock (anger management) returning back home. More than that, I learned a different way of life. I came back with a new set of eyes; a changed outlook. I thought missions was an opportunity to give, but honestly I received so much more than what I gave. I came home seeing the need in my own back yard. I was emboldened to share Christ with my own culture, to give of my time and treasures more freely, and to look for opportunities to serve others. Although the Thai culture was very different, I could now see that people have the same physical and spiritual needs everywhere. Really, missions is greatly misunderstood and if I could, I would change its advertising to this: Missions- trading in your old eyes for new and improved ones."

It's all about the relationship. We are shown by Christ over and over again that it is all about the relationship, not only with him but with other people. There is a need to be consistently in community to love those who do not want or feel they deserve love, and to be a voice to the voiceless. There are times also when the people we meet in life are often, I believe, placed there by God to challenge us, mold us or encourage us along our walk and to make a difference in our perspective and our passion for those in the world around us. I know that I would not be who I am today without the countless people who have joined me in my journey at all different times of my life. There are times when I did not want peoples' advices; other times when I craved it, and still others when God was calling me to be the advice giver. These different points in my life all lead to a place of better understanding and acknowledgment of who God is and what he wants us to do. It is through the people that I am able to see the love that God has for me but also the depth of sin that all have in our lives. People inspire us to go, to be and do what God is calling us to do and it is important that we follow where we feel led and not just follow the people. Oftentimes we have to break from the pack to find our own trails, and when this happens, God will be the best guide in making sure that you are where you need to be when you need to be there.

Dave S.

"My first mission trip changed my life. I went to communist Hungary in 1984 where we did evangelism with English speaking East European college students on their summer vacations. I remember meeting a guy from East Germany, which was staunchly atheistic at that time. I asked him what he thought of Jesus. He replied, "What is Jesus?" He did not even know Jesus existed or that he was a person. He had never heard the word before. I realized that God could use me in eternally significant ways if I would just step out and give him the opportunity.

I have often heard people skeptical that such random conversations make a real impact. While playing a pinball machine at a youth hostel that summer I met another student named Zoltan. He too had never heard the gospel, but was spiritually hungry and readily placed his faith in Christ. Twenty years later I got an email. It read, "You may not remember me but my name is Zoltan. You told me about Jesus twenty years ago and I became the first Christian in my family. Ever since I have been following him, and I just wanted you to know." Jesus said the kingdom of God is like a mustard seed that grows in and through us until it becomes a place where others find a home. One way to plant a mustard seed of faith is by going on a mission trip. All we have to do is step out and God does all the rest. We will never know until heaven all those who found a spiritual home in Christ because of our feeble and imperfect but divinely leveraged witness.

Sometimes we are so far away from God and we do not even realize it. It is within these moments that we find comfort when someone else intercedes on our behalf. We saw this with Miriam and Moses in the first part of the book and yet again in Matthew we have a man who steps out on faith in the middle of the crowd for his son that is demon possessed. The son does not ask for Jesus's help, but the father does. The demons are driven out and the boy is healed, but it is the onlookers who are taken aback by this message. We see in the next few verses the disciples are questioning Jesus about this healing and what it takes to have the power to heal in this capacity. Then we get the famous "faith of a mustard seed" verse. Seriously though, have you ever planted a mustard seed. They are TINY. I mean they are so small, yet eat mustard or watch the plant grow and you know that it does not take a bunch of something to make an impact. We see the change that we make on people many times years and years down the road if at all. It takes faith to keep making the impact on others, keep being that positive note in a world full of negative images and that kind voice in the midst of it all. Then maybe down the road we can see the legacy created in God's kingdom that God allowed us to be a part of. Only then can we see that our impacts are making a difference. What are you doing when nobody's watching? Is it reflecting Jesus?"

The anticipation that happens prior to a mission trip is something that cannot compare to anything that I can truly explain. There is something that is special about this time that you plan and pack certain items in your suitcase that will travel with you to a new and distant place. Yet there are things just like my blanket from the beginning that often act as comfort to you as you plan to get out of your comfort zone and embrace the unknown, usually with a bunch of people that you don't know the best, sharing really tight quarters or even beds in a place you have never been. It sounds like a wonderful start to a dream vacation, right? Well yes, actually in a way it is. There is something about the close quarters with people that brings you deep in a relationship with others way more than you thought would be possible in the span of a week or however long you are there. For some trips this anticipation makes me very giddy and excited. There is a hope and a longing of finding out what God is going to do and how he is going to be in the midst of it all that is almost the longing similar to the anticipation of Christmas and Christ's initial coming. This longing is much like this next story.

Lori W.

"Twas' the night before my very first mission trip. July 12, 2006, Honduras. C.A" That is the first line as I look back at my journal entries from dozens of past mission trips. I am overcome with emotion by the enthusiastic and passionate girl who wrote those words and these that followed. "Be the change you wish to see in the world" and four days into the mission trip "God, I feel like you are leading me to be an advocate. To be a voice for those who have no voice".

Here are a few scriptures I wrote down during those first 4 days on the mission trip: Micah 6:9 He has shown you, O mortal, what is good. And what does the Lord require of you? To act justly and to love mercy and to walk humbly with your God". Proverbs 31: "Speak up for those who cannot speak for themselves, for the rights of all who are destitute. Speak up and judge fairly; defend the rights of the poor and needy." Romans 10:14-15. "But how can they call on him to save them unless they believe in him? And how can they believe in him if they have never heard about him? And how can they hear about him unless someone tells them? And how will anyone go and tell them without being sent? That is why the Scriptures say, "How beautiful are the feet of messengers who bring good news!"

Looking back, I had no idea July 12, 2006 was the beginning of a new book in my life.

One filled with hope, love, sacrifice and service. I was 33, single and owned my own business as an interior designer. I always loved helping people, so when our church, The Cove, mentioned they were going on a mission trip to Honduras and were looking for people to go, I thought maybe that could be me?! I am a girlie girl, not much of the camper type, and fairly new to the Cove; but something about the invitation spoke to me. I had been preparing and serving lunch bi-monthly at the Mooresville Soup Kitchen and loved it, so I thought God uses me there he could use me in Honduras ...right?! July 13, 2006 we left for a 10-day mission trip and my life was never the same. How could I see and experience hurt, pain, poverty, yet love, beauty and God's grace and not be changed? I went on the trip expecting to help others which we did however there was another piece. God was preparing me and training me to take what I saw, learned and felt back home to my community, family, friends and really anyone who would listen. I prayed my first prayer out loud in a small church in Rio Bonito, mixed and poured concrete for a medical clinic, and looked into the eyes of children and shared the greatest story ever told! The story of Jesus, his love, sacrifice, hope and forgiveness. I came back from that trip and many others afterward with a burning desire and fire to keep the energy going. I could live every day as if I were on a mission trip. Just look around, I thought, we have the same needs and opportunities here in my backyard, community and even family. I proceeded to look for opportunities almost daily. I got more involved with the Mooresville Soup Kitchen, Habitat for Humanity, Women's Shelter and ultimately after months of praying, closed my interior design business and joined the staff at The Cove Church working in ministry full time. God cares more about our availability than our ability. I never really saw myself praying in public, sharing my testimony or being on staff at a church, where I had the amazing opportunity to lead others into a relationship with Christ. However, when we say YES to God and his plan, for us anything is possible. He will use us in our workplace, family, community and world to do extraordinary things.

Craig W.

It's funny how you mention the needs nearby. As I re- entered society I felt disjointed and out of sync. Is it me? This society? Or am I caught between two opposite worlds and not in either? I read something about the whole "leap of faith" ideal and that sometimes the faith part is telling you to stay put. God may have you where you are supposed to be and it is uncomfortable or not what you expected so you decide to change. The change is about you and your needs and not God's plan for your life.

I realize that my desire to help others is not mine. It is the Holy Spirit nudging me to do what I am here for. And it is very likely local in nature and not 1700 miles away.

I never took the time to look close by like I should have. Oh yeah, I gave the cursory glance and nodded and said " That's too bad, someone should help them". Then I could not let go of what I read and I think it's because I, yes I, am supposed to be listening to the Word and doing what We, the Holy Spirit and myself, are meant to do. So this year, and I don't do resolutions, I am hoping to do more locally and have an impact on the people here that need me and the Word in their lives.

My word this year is Trust, as in trust in the Lord with all you have and do. As such, it might take everyone around me to remind my A.D.D. self of this.

Corey R.

"Since a young age I've felt called into full-time ministry, meaning to pursue a career where my job's sole directive is to share the Gospel and make disciples. Some people think of this as what it means to be in missions, but I think we are all called and are qualified by the Gospel to be ambassadors of Christ and carry the message of the Gospel out to our sphere of influence, be that our workplace, coffee group, sports team, etc.

In high school I was involved in the International Baccalaureate (IB) Program. This program required us to have a certain number of community service hours for graduation. As a result, I got plugged in with Habitat for Humanity. At first it was a chore, but I quickly fell in love with it. That's probably where my heart for service first originated. While in college I had been involved with Cru at UNC-Wilmington (my alma mater) and went to our winter conference "Encounter." It was there that I heard the testimony of a woman who had come from East Asia and described the persecution for their faith. I was moved, but it wasn't until a mentor of mine challenged me to go on a short summer mission trip junior year that I considered leaving. I have to admit, sure part of my reasoning was it'd be cool to see God use me there, but my primary motivation was to travel and experience a different culture. That and I knew I loved Asian food! Little did I know God would use that summer to open my eyes and develop a global vision for His Kingdom. While there I had the privilege of witnessing a student come to Christ, and as I heard him pray in his own dialect, I could not help but form an image of every tribe, tongue, nation, united in worshiping God. After spending time in Asia and then returning back to the United States, I knew God was calling me back. After finishing my degree at UNC-Wilmington I came on staff with Cru and returned to Asia to serve for a year and a half. What I did not realize was how God would use me to work in the lives around me, but also to work in my own life opening myself to new opportunities and possibilities that I never would have noticed before missions.

It's very eye opening returning home. You have a whole new perspective and the world just isn't the same. This was most indicative of me when I returned home from my first summer mission trip. God had used that summer to completely rip open my eyes and awaken my heart, so when I returned to America and found it the same, I felt terribly lonely. At times I wanted to shout and scream, but resolved to crying because I knew I couldn't blame my friends and family. If I did at best, I'd sound vain. Eventually, I began seeking opportunities to lovingly encourage others through the stories and experiences God has blessed me with. I'm still working it out honestly!

I had a number of misconceptions going into full-time ministry, particularly in the level of challenges that would be involved. From support-raising to on the field in full-time ministry, the Lord worked more in my heart in these past couple years than in my entire life combined. Daily sharing and looking for opportunities to spread the Gospel, and asking those who could be persecuted just for having faith caused me to question if I really believed what I was sharing. Being in this environment brought me to a point where I had to do a lot of self-analyzation, and left me with a genuine faith in the Lord that has become my foundation. Biblically, we are all called to live on mission, no matter where we are. This can look like serving our neighbors and co-workers to local community development, to being sent to the furthest corners of the earth. Missions is simply being "doers" of the Word and not just readers or listeners, as referred to in the book of James.

Going on mission overseas also gave me balance between really having an appreciation for the great things about my country while simultaneously more aware of our flaws. There's some things you are relieved to return to. There are also things, people, food dishes, sights, cultural norms that are gut-wrenching to leave behind in the mission field.

Seeing people come together in a culture completely different than your own has an impact on your heart. You begin to see God's supremacy. Specifically, how people of another culture can connect to God and worship Him for completely unique aspects that I in America would never have thought to appreciate. It's empowering to see how God is alive and active meeting each of us where we are in our lives.

Serving abroad certainly had its difficulties, especially when I had committed to stay there long-term. Suddenly, all those little quirky weird things I was amused with on a short-term trip became something I would be forced to live with indefinitely. There's extremely challenging aspects to adapting to a new culture and language, finding out what's proper and what's offensive, how to get around, how to order food, even how to use the bathroom.

I personally found living abroad in Asia a blessing. I thrived in the new environment and was continually thrilled by new experiences and encounters. Even when the thrill started to go away, Asia started to feel like home. However, ministry continued to be a difficult task. Though I could help bridge the gap with better language, and becoming more culturally assimilated, I would always be an outsider. This really challenged me about how I used my time and engaged in ministry back in the States. In America I've often been fearful of what people will think. Our team in Asia had a saying "everything is awkward so nothing is awkward." In Asia we already knew we were outsiders so we weren't afraid to look foolish. But in America, where I speak the language fluently, understand the culture, and can have long-lasting relationships, I've been less willing to step out of my comfort zone. This was very convicting to me.

When I came back I definitely wanted to serve more. Perhaps the best way to phrase it is to serve better and more intelligently. I found myself initially rushing into it thinking I would save the world and faced a harsh reality of the brokenness within the world. But through the grind God really transformed me and those around me. There's no doubt that ministry can be draining, especially as it refines you and sorts through your heart and motivations, but there's been absolutely nothing more rewarding than drawing closer to the Lord as a result.

If you are interested in serving, look for opportunities to serve in your local communities. A great place to start is with your church. Ask around and see where other people are serving. If you can't find any or one that interests you, look into local non-profits; there are a number of them that do incredible work right in your own backyard. While serving, intentionally look for opportunities to step out, have conversations, and build relationships with people in the community.

If you want to go abroad, again start with the church. See if they are planning or know of any organizations leading a trip. Every trip will look a lot different based on the culture you will be entering into, the team you go with, and the service your group hopes to provide. Pray about it and try to find one that you feel the Lord leading you most to. If you have the opportunity, by all means go!

No matter where you serve you are making a difference; if you allow Him, God will use it to change your heart as well!"

From Corey's international experience and the call on his life others are impacted internationally in a different way. Questions about local service, and continuous actions needed where you already have a strong network and resources are often raised. Why there? Why not here?

Chris C.

"Technically, the only international mission trip I have been on was more of a service learning project. It's also been awhile since I've been on the non-helping organize things side of any mission trip. But to reach back in my memory, whenever I have been on mission trips, I have always wondered "Why not at home?" That's something that I always wanted in high school with our annual trips, but my shy, introverted self never had the guts to say anything. I think that, as long as those leading the trips do a good job of reinforcing that mission is a way of life rather than a trip, then people would want to serve more locally. I wanted to serve locally when I came home. Unfortunately, especially when I was younger, I had no idea where or how to serve. I think there's a willingness there with people, but they don't know how to go about it."

These stories are so inspiring. Networks of resources are needed locally and abroad so we too can join in the beautiful work that God has gifted each one of us to do. These thoughts in the back of our minds may often be pushed aside because of our poor planning and lack of priorities. It may be because we just don't know how to start. I pray that this does not stop us from trying.

You may be looking at your list thinking my list is too short, I can't do anything with the skill set that I have I make (insert your current occupation) for a living and that is not a ministry. I want to challenge you in this area, just like any job application we write on our resume the skills in which we have that relate to the job that is posted. Sometimes we are lucky enough to have titles that say something similar to the new job position that we are hoping to gain; other times we have to pull from our resources and be "resourceful" in thinking of ways to use our management of our house to translate to management of people. You have more skills than you often recognize.

So you have the list in front you, great. Now do something with it. This is easier said than done. Just like the resume, if there is a ministry option out there that already fits one of your passions and resources, jump in with that organization. Don't be afraid to be honest if you are initially not sure if it is the right fit for you, and tell the organization up front that you are looking to help them and see how the organization works from the inside out. Humans are most likely to pick one organization a year to put their time money and resources into. If you are an organization, you want to make sure you are good but as a possible volunteer / resource, you want to make sure you fit also. Second, here comes the hard part, there may not be an organization that fits the passion that you have or the resources that you have…

I have had the amazing privilege to work with many organizations within my community all during, prior and after my foreign mission trips. By being associated with them I have an immediate connection that I can pour into once I land back home when the Jesus "high" that you get on mission trips is still there and it can be immediately used to touch someone's life. One thing I often regret is waiting to do something for so long that when I finally get the courage to do it, the opportunity is no longer there or someone else has been bold enough to do so. We need not to be pushy when we come home but there is always room and need for passion in each organization.

I bet you are thinking at this point there is not an organization out there that does what I want to do with people in my community. First of all, I would challenge you with that notion. I have found just by continuous asking and networking there are more nonprofits and organizations here in my small town than I ever thought possible. If you have conducted this search and to no avail the type of organization that you are looking for is not there, I offer you two options. I would first expand your search, is there an organization within 30 minutes instead of only within 10 that does what you are looking for? Do they need help? (which again I would argue yes, in almost any organization). The best resource a nonprofit has is the people in which they serve, that serve and those that know about what they do. For it is these people who make the organization run. They are the doers, movers and shakers and they make things happen. They also are a walking marketing mechanism. If the organization is doing something amazing people will know; if they are not, people will know. Just ask.

The second option that I suggest is look even further. You may be thinking that this is a no brainer, however it doesn't really make sense to look at an organization in Ohio for ideas about an organization in North Carolina. You might be surprised. The current trend is organizations are looking for people all over to work with them and spread what they do. I have a friend who works for an organization that is a sub organization of a non-profit out of _____. They do amazing work. Yes, he did have to start the organization but drafting the mission, vision, and many of the structure and functions of the organization that initially takes so long to get in place, approved and accepted were already done and now his organization in thriving in Charlotte helping students in an afterschool program and empowering the students as they move up in their school to become leaders within the program itself. It is amazing to see what looking and talking to people can do.

Many organizations may want to do something that is a little different from what they are doing now that still remains in their mission and vision, but do not have the staff or the time to develop a program. Talk with the leaders of the organization to see if they would be interested in creating an initiative that would cover your passions. Many times if their organization cannot support your passion, good leaders will direct you to another organization who possibly could.

I say it all the time that I love conferences, but seriously, go to conferences. They can inspire you to live out your mission experience both locally and globally. Go to local, regional and national conferences if at all possible. If funds are a problem, hopefully you are already working with and volunteering for a non-profit, ask and see which conferences they are interested in attending and if they are having a booth. If they do, work the booth, and then as you are talking with other people as they are walking around use your words and network.

I know we have cell phones these days and the wonderful yet often terrible thing called the internet, yet nothing even if it is awkward beats a face to face conversation with someone. It is these moments that you can make connections to things that you want to steer clear from they can tell you their successes and failures and you can each begin to walk together on the journey of impacting people wherever you are.

"Your current direction will determine your destination. And like every principle, you can leverage this one to your advantage or ignore it to your disadvantage. Just as there are paths that have led us to places we never intended to be, there are paths that lead us away from those places as well"[14]

---

[14] *The Principle of the Path*, Andy Stanley.

Next Steps

I have been able to see how helping one another financially and prayerfully has made all the difference in the trips we have taken. From firsthand experience I have been amazed time and time again to be on the receiving end of both prayer and support. Though many times unspoken, these words of encouragement and strength and the glimmer of hope when I was beginning to think that my flame was fading, created a revival that lasted longer than anything I could have said or done in that moment.

This is where you come in.

I have partnered with a great organization called Above and Beyond, and their mission is to serve locally to go globally. They help provide scholarships for people going on mission trips by the participants serving locally in their community for an approved number of hours and earning up to a fourth of their trip expenses covered by the organization. They helped fund me on one of my trips. When I thought it was going to be very difficult to make the payments, their support created all the difference that I needed to look forward to the trip without the stress of the finances. I was able to serve in locations around the community where I was able to meet people that I now see on a weekly basis and develop relationships with them as we together impact the community for a greater good.

Just like Above and Beyond, one fourth of the proceeds from this book will be donated back to this organization to help other people have an easier time to serve locally and go globally and to truly in every way shape and for Go Away Closer. Check them out at aboveandbeyond.cc to find out more.

Thank you for being the hands and feet of Christ and may he bless you on each journey as you Go AWAY Closer.

Elizabeth

Organizations

Do you have an organization that is doing something well? I would love to hear about it! Post it and let us know where it is and what the people are doing. How are they serving the lost, hurt, and least, of these and what difference are they making? I know and see so many organizations that are out there doing great things. I have heard through the grapevine stories of the small town rising above, the NFL player coming from the underdog league, the stories highlighted on CNN, ABC, NBC and on the latest talk shows. But stories are happening all around us that are under the radar. The boy who never had any family member even apply to college because they didn't even finish high school is now not just a college student, but a summa cum laude graduate. The person, who despite physical disabilities, did something that people never thought possible. The moment that someone was given a dream and they, for the first time, actually thought that it could become a reality. These moments happen within non-profits local and abroad. It takes that one moment within the local small group at church, or one moment when a mission trip is offered and there is a scholarship to go. I want to hear about these stories and how they impacted someone in going, either away or closer.

The last thing that an organization is going to do is put money into marketing and advertising when it can put money into programs and services. However, without volunteering with them or working with the organization in some capacity, the curtains are drawn and no one realizes the impact that they are making.

It is my hope that through this book you think about passion differently, that you see missions as both local and global, and that you act in both ways. I hope that you see church as an avenue to organizations that are doing something well, and that you can communicate with non-profits in your areas, sharing services and resources so that you become more like the body of Christ and less burned out. I pray that as some collaborations do not work, that you agree to disagree and you maintain a Christ-like attitude as you work through the mess and possibly even break up a partnership that you thought and prayed was going to work. It is my prayer that you would be willing to collaborate again, that you open yourself up to where, when and how God is leading you in every aspect of your life, business, home, career and family, and that through God's prompting, you follow where he leads.

Now it's your turn!

GO AWAY CLOSER

Bibliography

"2013 Vacation Deprivation Study." Expedia Viewfinder. 2013. Web. 31 Jan. 2015.

Caine, Christine. *Undaunted: Daring to Do What God Calls You to Do.* Grand Rapids, Michigan: Zondervan, 2012. Print.

Fuder, John. *A Heart for the City: Effective Ministries to the Urban Community.* Chicago, IL: Moody, 1999. Print.

Guillebeau, Chris. "A Brief Guide to World Domination." World Domination. 2008. Web.

People Groups. Web. 1 May 2011. https://www.peoplegroups.info/search/Default .aspx?SC=ny>.

"The Top 5 Most Expensive Hurricanes In U.S. History." Fortune The Top 5 Most Expensive Hurricanes in US History Comments. 2015. Web. 31 Jan. 2015.

Wikipedia. Wikimedia Foundation. Web. 2 May 2011. <http://en.wikipedia.org/wiki/Demographics_of_New_York_City>.

Wilson, Pete. *Plan B: What Do You Do When God Doesn't Show up the Way You Thought He Would?* Nashville, TN: Thomas Nelson, 2009. Print.

www.ingramcontent.com/pod-product-compliance
Lightning Source LLC
Chambersburg PA
CBHW071718090426
42738CB00009B/1813